LOW-FAT
WAYS TO
BAKE

COMPILED AND EDITED BY
SUSAN M. McINTOSH, M.S., R.D.

Oxmoor House®

Copyright 1998 by Oxmoor House, Inc.
Book Division of Southern Progress Corporation
P.O. Box 2463, Birmingham, Alabama 35201

Library of Congress Catalog Number: 97-76299
ISBN: 0-8487-2216-7
Manufactured in the United States of America
First Printing 1998

Editor-in-Chief: Nancy Fitzpatrick Wyatt
Editorial Director, Special Interest Publications: Ann H. Harvey
Senior Foods Editor: Katherine M. Eakin
Senior Editor, Editorial Services: Olivia Kindig Wells
Art Director: James Boone

LOW-FAT WAYS TO BAKE

Menu and Recipe Consultant: Susan McEwen McIntosh, M.S., R.D.
Assistant Editor: Kelly Hooper Troiano
Associate Foods Editor: Anne Chappell Cain, M.S., M.P.H., R.D.
Copy Editor: Keri Bradford Anderson
Editorial Assistant: Meredith V. Mathis
Indexer: Mary Ann Laurens
Associate Art Director: Cynthia R. Cooper
Designer: Carol Damsky
Senior Photographer: Jim Bathie
Photographers: Howard L. Puckett, *Cooking Light* magazine;
  Ralph Anderson, Brit Huckabay; Tim Turner (page 101)
Senior Photo Stylist: Kay E. Clarke
Photo Stylists: Cindy Manning Barr, *Cooking Light* magazine;
  Virginia R. Cravens
Production Director: Phillip Lee
Associate Production Manager: Vanessa Cobbs Richardson
Production Assistant: Faye Porter Bonner

> ### We're Here for You!
>
> We at Oxmoor House are
> dedicated to serving you with
> reliable information that expands
> your imagination and enriches your
> life. We welcome your comments
> and suggestions. Please write us at:
>
> Oxmoor House, Inc.
> Editor, *Low-Fat Ways To Bake*
> 2100 Lakeshore Drive
> Birmingham, AL 35209

Our appreciation to the staff of *Cooking Light* magazine and to the Southern
Progress Corporation library staff for their contributions to this book.

Cover (clockwise from top): *Sour Cream-Lemon Pound Cake (page 87),
Blueberry-Oat Streusel Muffins (page 33), and Cinnamon Swirl Bread (page 59)*
Frontispiece: *Harvest Bread (page 61)*

CONTENTS

READY, SET, BAKE!

*N*othing offers comfort quite like freshly baked breads, cookies, cakes, and pies. And when these homemade treats are both healthy and delicious, everyone will be satisfied. Preparing great-tasting breads and desserts low in fat and calories is easy, once you learn a few low-fat baking basics.

Start with an easy muffin, or jump right into yeast bread or a fancy pastry. Either way, the recipes in this book are guaranteed to satisfy.

Bread recipes make up the first four chapters. Flip through these pages, and you'll find quick recipes for biscuits, scones, muffins, and cornbreads as well as recipes for traditional yeast breads. The remaining sections are devoted to desserts, from supereasy recipes such as Chocolate Cream Cupcakes (page 76) to more sophisticated specialties such as Lemon Cheesecake (page 130).

Before you heat up the oven, check out your kitchen for the proper equipment. Also, take a moment to familiarize yourself with several basic ingredients and measuring techniques used to prepare both breads and desserts.

EQUIPMENT

You can make your baking much easier by having the proper cooking tools. Buy the best kitchen equipment you can afford; sturdier products last longer and perform better.

Some of the equipment you need in your kitchen includes mixing bowls in various sizes; liquid and dry measuring cups; measuring spoons; mixing spoons; a pastry blender; a rolling pin; a sifter; rubber and metal spatulas; a thermometer; a timer; a wire whisk; and wire cooling racks.

If you bake a lot, you also need several sizes and types of baking sheets, loafpans, and specialty baking pans. Select high-quality pans and baking sheets for long-term use. Shiny aluminum is a good choice for most baked goods. For pies, use ovenproof glass or dull metal piepans. Insulated pans and pans with nonstick dark surfaces are also available. Insulated pans may require longer baking times, while foods baked in pans with dark surfaces brown more quickly. (Check manufacturer's instructions for adjusting baking temperatures and times.)

For best results, use the size pan called for in the recipe. If you don't have the correct size, try one of the pan substitutions suggested in the chart below. But be aware that when you substitute a pan that holds the same amount but is a different shape, the recipe's cooking time will vary. Generally, the deeper the pan, the longer the cooking time.

PAN SUBSTITUTIONS	
Recipe calls for:	Substitute:
8-inch round pan	10- x 6- x 2-inch pan
8-inch square pan	11- x 7- x 1½-inch pan
9-inch square pan	9- x 5- x 3-inch loafpan or two 8-inch round pans
13- x 9- x 2-inch pan	two 9-inch round pans or three 8-inch round pans
10-inch tube pan	two 9- x 5- x 3-inch loafpans

INGREDIENTS

Baking recipes usually have a few basic ingredients in common. Here is an explanation of some of these and what they do.

Popovers (page 31) are leavened by eggs and the steam created by an initially high oven temperature.

• **Baking powder** is often used to leaven quick breads, cakes, and cookies. Double-acting baking powder is the most common type. When mixed with liquid, it starts producing gases to make the batter or dough rise; it reacts again when heated during baking. Baking powder is perishable, so be sure to use it before the expiration date on the can. You can test its effectiveness by combining 1 teaspoon baking powder with ⅓ cup hot water; the baking powder should bubble vigorously. A suitable substitute for 1 teaspoon baking powder is ¼ teaspoon baking soda plus ½ teaspoon cream of tartar.

• **Baking soda,** another common leavener, starts reacting as soon as it is combined with a liquid. For that reason, bake batters containing baking soda right after mixing together dry and liquid ingredients.

• **Chocolate,** a favorite dessert ingredient, comes in many forms—including unsweetened cocoa, semisweet chocolate, unsweetened chocolate, milk chocolate, and sweet baking chocolate. Unsweetened cocoa is lowest in fat. You can substitute cocoa for unsweetened chocolate. The general guideline is to use 3 tablespoons cocoa plus 1 tablespoon melted margarine for each ounce of unsweetened chocolate. (You may omit the margarine to cut fat.)

• **Eggs** provide structure to baked products and incorporate air bubbles into the batter. Eggs are available in several sizes. The size makes little difference in taste, but recipes in the *Low-Fat Ways To Cook* series are based on large eggs. Each large egg measures about ¼ cup.

An egg white contains no fat or cholesterol, but a large egg yolk has about 213 milligrams of cholesterol and 5 grams of fat. Many of the recipes in this book call for two egg whites in place of a whole egg to lower cholesterol and fat. Others specify fat-free egg substitute, which contains no cholesterol. When modifying your own recipes, use ¼ cup egg substitute for each whole egg.

• **Fat** of some type helps tenderize, provides volume, and adds flavor to baked goods. Fats traditionally used in baking (butter, shortening, and lard) are high in saturated fat and cholesterol. However, you often can use margarine or vegetable oil instead to lower the saturated fat and cholesterol content.

When selecting a stick margarine, make sure that the amount of saturated fat is 2 grams or less per tablespoon. Recommended oils include canola, olive, peanut, safflower, sunflower, corn, and soybean.

Stay away from reduced-calorie margarines and spreads when baking. They may be low in saturated fat, but they usually have too much water and too little fat to produce the correct results in baked foods.

• **Flour** can be made from different grains, such as wheat, rye, oats, and barley. Each flour has unique characteristics based on the grain used and the degree of milling. The most frequently called-for flour is all-purpose. Most all-purpose flour is bleached—or whitened—during processing. Unbleached flour may be used interchangeably with all-purpose flour.

Self-rising flour is simply all-purpose flour with an added leavening agent and salt. Although it is not suitable for yeast breads, it is often called for in recipes for biscuits and other quick breads. (One cup self-rising flour equals 1 cup all-purpose flour plus 1 teaspoon baking powder and ½ teaspoon salt.)

Bread flour is ideal for yeast breads because when stirred with water and kneaded, it develops a high gluten content. Gluten gives elasticity to dough and provides the structure for baked foods.

Cake flour produces a very tender, delicate texture and therefore is recommended for many cakes. Always sift cake flour before measuring it. (If a recipe calls for 1 cup sifted cake flour, you can substitute 1 cup minus 2 tablespoons sifted all-purpose flour.)

Cake flour is used in Sour Cream-Lemon Pound Cake (page 87) to produce a tender, delicate texture.

Whole wheat flour contains wheat germ, giving it a higher fiber content than white flour. Refrigerate whole wheat flour to keep it from becoming rancid.

• **Milk** or a milk product is often the liquid of choice to mix with the dry ingredients. Whole milk and products made from it are high in fat, especially saturated fat. When a recipe calls for whole milk or cream, try substituting reduced-fat (2%), low-fat (1%), or fat-free (skim) milk. Substitute nonfat or low-fat sour cream for its higher-fat counterpart. Choose nonfat yogurt instead of that made from whole milk.

Keep nonfat dry milk powder on hand to use as a substitute for milk in baked goods. Reconstituted dry buttermilk powder is equally effective as a substitute for fresh buttermilk.

• **Salt** improves the taste and works with yeast in leavening yeast breads. Flavor is salt's only purpose in cookies, cakes, and pastries.

• **Sugar and other sweeteners** define desserts, but breads also benefit from the addition of sugar. It adds taste and has the ability to tenderize. Sugar also contributes to the browning process of crusts. Granulated sugar is the most common form of sugar and the kind used when sugar is specified in this book's recipes. Other sweeteners include powdered sugar, brown sugar, molasses, honey, and corn syrup.

• **Yeast** is essential to yeast breads because of its leavening ability. It is actually a type of bacteria that multiplies and grows when exposed to moisture and food (sugar or starch) in a warm place.

The recipes in this book call for dry yeast—either active dry yeast or rapid-rise yeast. You usually can substitute rapid-rise yeast in equal amounts for active dry yeast by following the package directions; the rising time will be reduced by about half. Dry yeast is perishable; use it before the expiration date on the package. Store yeast in a cool, dry place. You also can store it in the refrigerator or freezer; just bring the yeast to room temperature before using it in a recipe. (See facing page for more about baking with yeast.)

Make It Easy

When you want steaming hot bread for dinner but are really short on time, think convenience. Just keep several quick-fix bread products on hand, such as reduced-fat biscuit and baking mix, frozen bread dough, refrigerated French bread dough, and hot roll mix. With a pinch of this and a dab of that, you can have fresh bread on the dinner table in no time!

Refrigerated dough makes Lemon-Glazed Cranberry Rolls (page 51) especially quick.

THE MAGIC OF YEAST

Yeast bread has a reputation for being difficult to make. But there's no mystery to baking beautiful yeast bread once you are familiar with these steps.

• **Dissolving.** Most recipes require that you activate the yeast by dissolving it in warm water (105° to 115°) before adding any other ingredients. Water that is too hot will kill the yeast, while water that is too cool will make the bread slow to rise. Use a candy or yeast thermometer for accuracy.

After you dissolve the yeast in a warm liquid (usually with some sugar), let it stand in a warm place 5 to 10 minutes. Yeast that is alive will swell and bubble slightly. If nothing happens, the yeast is probably dead—start over with a new package.

Some breads follow the rapid-mix method, in which the undissolved yeast is mixed with some of the dry ingredients before adding liquids. With this method, the liquid should be 120° to 130° when added to the dry ingredients unless otherwise noted.

• **Kneading.** Gluten develops after flour is mixed with water and the dough is kneaded. Kneading strengthens the elastic structure of the dough.

To knead, turn the dough out onto a lightly floured surface. Using lightly floured hands, lift the edge of the dough farthest from you and fold it toward you. Using the heels of both hands, press down into the dough and away from you. Give the dough a quarter turn. Fold the dough toward you again; repeat the kneading procedure until the dough begins to feel smooth and elastic. Continue

Knead dough until it's smooth and elastic.

adding flour in small amounts until the dough loses its stickiness; on humid days you will need to add more flour. Kneading can take up to 10 minutes.

• **Rising.** The ideal rising temperature for yeast dough is 85°. Place the dough in a gas oven with the pilot light on, in an electric oven with the oven light on, or in an oven containing a large pan of hot water. Each place should provide the right temperature as well as a draft-free environment.

Rising is complete when the dough has doubled in bulk, unless the recipe specifies otherwise. To test the dough for doubled bulk, lightly press a finger ½ inch into the dough. If the indentation

Test for doubled bulk before shaping the dough.

remains, the dough has risen enough and is ready to shape. To make dough ahead of time, let it rise in the refrigerator. It will take about eight hours to rise at this cooler temperature; it will keep up to five days if made with water or three days if made with milk. Punch the dough down each day.

• **Shaping.** After the dough has risen once, it is ready to be shaped into loaves, rolls, or other types of bread. Turn the dough out onto a floured surface. Cover and let it rest 5 to 10 minutes before shaping. This allows the gluten to relax, making the dough softer and easier to handle. In most cases, you will allow the shaped dough to rise again before baking.

• **Baking.** Bake most breads in the center of a preheated oven with space around pans so that heat can circulate freely. Yeast loaves are done if they sound hollow when tapped lightly with your knuckles. Cover bread loosely with aluminum foil if it starts to get too brown before baking is complete.

Remove bread from pans immediately after baking. Cool baked loaves on a wire rack to prevent the crust from becoming soggy.

HOW TO MEASURE

For your recipes to turn out the way you want, you must measure ingredients accurately. Not all ingredients are measured the same way or in the same type of measuring utensil. Learn to measure the right way with the proper equipment.

• **What to use.** Measure liquids in glass or clear plastic measuring cups with a rim above the last cup level to prevent spilling. Liquid measuring cups are available in 1-cup, 2-cup, and 4-cup sizes. Measure dry ingredients in metal or plastic graduated dry-measuring cups in 1-cup, ½-cup, ⅓-cup, and ¼-cup sizes.

When measuring liquid or dry ingredients in amounts less than ¼ cup, use measuring spoons in 1-tablespoon, 1-teaspoon, ½-teaspoon, and ¼-teaspoon sizes. (One-fourth cup equals 4 tablespoons, and a dash equals ¹⁄₁₆ teaspoon.)

• **Measuring liquids.** To measure liquids correctly, place the cup on a level surface. Get eye level with the marking you want to read, and fill the cup to that line. (For ease of reading, open your upper cabinet door, and place the cup on the shelf nearest eye level.)

Place a liquid measuring cup on a level surface when measuring liquids.

To measure a small amount of a thin liquid, pour it into the appropriate measuring spoon until full. Pour a thick liquid into the measuring spoon until full; then level it.

• **Measuring dry ingredients.** To measure dry ingredients, lightly spoon (not scoop) the ingredient into the cup or measuring spoon, letting it mound; then level the top with a flat edge, such as a metal or plastic spatula, to achieve a smooth surface. Never pack dry ingredients—except brown sugar. It needs to be packed firmly enough so that the sugar keeps the shape of the measuring cup when it's turned out.

When measuring dried herbs, keep as close to level as possible.

Lightly spoon flour into the measuring cup; then level the top with a flat edge.

• **Measuring other ingredients.** Use a dry-measuring cup to measure shortening. Pack it tightly to eliminate air bubbles; then level it. Butter and margarine often are already measured. You usually can follow the marks on the wrapper for a certain number of tablespoons or fraction of a cup.

To Sift or Not to Sift

Most brands of flour today are presifted, so it's no longer necessary to sift before measuring. Stir the flour to lighten it; then gently spoon it into the proper dry-measuring cup, and level it. Don't shake the cup to level it because you'll pack the flour. The exceptions to the no-sift rule are cake flour and powdered sugar, which are very soft and tend to pack down during storage. Sift them; then measure as directed above.

LOW-FAT BASICS

*W*hether you are trying to lose or maintain weight, low-fat eating makes good sense. Research studies show that decreasing your fat intake reduces risks of heart disease, diabetes, and some types of cancer. The goal recommended by major health groups is an intake of 30 percent or less of total daily calories.

The *Low-Fat Ways To Cook* series gives you practical, delicious recipes with realistic advice about low-fat cooking and eating. The recipes are lower in total fat than traditional recipes. In fact, most provide less than 30 percent from fat and less than 10 percent from saturated fat.

Food Processor Pastry on page 113 is an exception. Although lower in fat than a standard recipe, this pastry receives 39 percent of its calories from fat. But when the pastry is combined with a low-fat filling, the recipe as a whole may be within the recommended percentage of fat. For example, Spiced Pumpkin Pie on page 115 calls for Food Processor Pastry with a low-fat pumpkin filling. When the total pie is analyzed, fat contributes only 19 percent of the calories.

The goal of fat reduction is not to eliminate fat entirely. In fact, a small amount of fat is needed to transport fat-soluble vitamins and maintain other normal body functions.

FIGURING THE FAT

The easiest way to achieve a diet with 30 percent or fewer of total calories from fat is to establish a daily "fat budget" based on the total number of calories you need each day. Multiply your current weight by 15 to estimate your daily calorie requirements. Remember that calorie requirements vary according to age, body size, and level of activity. To gain or lose 1 pound a week, add or subtract 500 calories a day. (A diet of fewer than 1,200 calories is not recommended unless medically supervised.)

To calculate your recommended fat allowance, multiply your daily calorie needs by .30 and divide by 9 (the number of calories in each gram of fat). You daily fat gram intake should not exceed this number. For quick reference, see the Daily Fat Limits Chart.

DAILY FAT LIMITS

Calories Per Day	30 Percent of Calories	Grams of Fat
1,200	360	40
1,500	450	50
1,800	540	60
2,000	600	67
2,200	660	73
2,500	750	83
2,800	840	93

NUTRITIONAL ANALYSIS

Each recipe in *Low-Fat Ways To Bake* has been kitchen-tested by a staff of food professionals. In addition, registered dietitians have determined the nutrient information using a computer system that analyzes every ingredient. These efforts ensure the success of each recipe and will help you fit these recipes into your own meal planning.

The nutrient grid that follows each recipe provides calories per serving and the percentage of calories from fat. In addition, the grid lists the grams of total fat, saturated fat, protein, and carbohydrate, and the milligrams of cholesterol and sodium per serving. The nutrient values are as accurate as possible and are based on these assumptions.

• When a range is given for an ingredient (3 to 3½ cups, for instance), the lesser amount is calculated.

• When a recipe calls for "margarine," the analysis is based on regular stick margarine. If "reduced-calorie margarine" is specified, the analysis is based on reduced-calorie stick margarine, not the kind in a tube or squeeze bottle.

• Garnishes and other optional ingredients are not calculated.

• Recipes calling for eggs or egg whites were tested with and analyzed for large eggs or egg whites.

• Some of the alcohol calories evaporate during heating, and only those remaining are counted.

• Fruits and vegetables listed in the ingredients are not peeled unless specified.

Strawberry-Pecan Scones (recipe on page 21)

BISCUITS, SCONES & CRACKERS

*Q*uick breads are just that—quick! They require no rising time and little, if any, kneading. This chapter offers you an assortment of easy quick breads including biscuits. Often containing only five or six ingredients, biscuits can usually be prepared and baked in less than 20 minutes.

Scones, a bread native to Scotland, are similar to biscuits, both in ingredients and the techniques used to prepare them. Traditionally, scones were slightly sweet and made with oats. Today's scones may or may not call for oats and can be sweet or savory. Follow the tips on page 20 to ensure success with your homemade biscuits and scones.

Closing out the chapter are recipes for biscotti and several crackers. Try them as appetizers, snacks, or accompaniments to soups and salads.

EASY BUTTERMILK BISCUITS

2 cups all-purpose flour
2 teaspoons baking powder
¼ teaspoon baking soda
¼ teaspoon salt
3 tablespoons plus 1 teaspoon chilled stick
    margarine, cut into small pieces
¾ cup 1% low-fat buttermilk

Combine first 4 ingredients in a large bowl; cut in margarine with a pastry blender until mixture resembles coarse meal. Add buttermilk, stirring just until dry ingredients are moistened.

Turn dough out onto a floured surface; knead 4 or 5 times. Roll dough to ½-inch thickness; cut into rounds with a 2½-inch biscuit cutter. Place rounds on a baking sheet. Bake at 450° for 12 minutes or until golden. Yield: 1 dozen.

PER BISCUIT: 112 CALORIES (29% FROM FAT)
FAT 3.6G (SATURATED FAT 0.7G)
PROTEIN 2.7G CARBOHYDRATE 16.8G
CHOLESTEROL 0MG SODIUM 161MG

BACON-CORNMEAL BISCUITS

The margarine is easier to cut into the dry ingredients if first cut into small pieces.

1¼ cups self-rising flour
1 cup self-rising cornmeal
1 tablespoon brown sugar
⅛ teaspoon ground red pepper
3 tablespoons chilled stick margarine, cut into
    small pieces
3 slices turkey bacon, cooked and crumbled
⅔ cup nonfat buttermilk
2 teaspoons self-rising flour
Vegetable cooking spray

Combine first 4 ingredients in a large bowl; cut in margarine with a pastry blender until mixture resembles coarse meal. Stir in turkey bacon. Add buttermilk, stirring with a fork just until dry ingredients are moistened.

Sprinkle 2 teaspoons flour evenly over work surface. Turn dough out onto floured surface; knead 8 to 10 times. Roll dough to ½-inch thickness; cut into rounds with a 2-inch biscuit cutter. Place rounds on a baking sheet coated with cooking spray. Bake at 400° for 14 minutes or until golden. Serve warm. Yield: 15 biscuits.

PER BISCUIT: 98 CALORIES (28% FROM FAT)
FAT 3.1G (SATURATED FAT 0.6G)
PROTEIN 2.5G CARBOHYDRATE 14.8G
CHOLESTEROL 2MG SODIUM 316MG

SWEET POTATO BISCUITS

For tender biscuits, follow the techniques shown on the facing page for cutting margarine into the dry ingredients.

2 cups all-purpose flour
1 tablespoon baking powder
¼ teaspoon salt
2 tablespoons brown sugar
3 tablespoons plus 1 teaspoon chilled stick
    margarine, cut into small pieces
¾ cup 1% low-fat milk
½ cup cooked, mashed sweet potato

Combine first 4 ingredients in a large bowl; cut in margarine with a pastry blender until mixture resembles coarse meal. Add milk and sweet potato; stir just until dry ingredients are moistened.

Turn dough out onto a heavily floured surface; knead 4 or 5 times. Roll dough to ½-inch thickness; cut into rounds with a 2½-inch biscuit cutter. Place rounds on a baking sheet. Bake at 450° for 15 minutes or until golden. Yield: 1 dozen.

PER BISCUIT: 131 CALORIES (25% FROM FAT)
FAT 3.6G (SATURATED FAT 0.8G)
PROTEIN 2.9G CARBOHYDRATE 21.6G
CHOLESTEROL 1MG SODIUM 171MG

From left: *Sweet Potato Biscuits and Sour Cream and Chive Biscuits (recipe on page 16)*

For Sweet Potato Biscuits, cut margarine into dry ingredients with a pastry blender until mixture resembles coarse meal.

Add milk and sweet potato; stir just until moistened. Turn dough out onto a floured surface; knead 4 or 5 times.

Roll dough to $^1/_2$-inch thickness; cut dough with $2^1/_2$-inch biscuit cutter. Place rounds on a baking sheet.

BUCKWHEAT BISCUITS

*Toasted kasha adds a slightly nutty
flavor to these hearty biscuits.*

1¾ cups all-purpose flour
1 tablespoon baking powder
¼ teaspoon baking soda
¼ teaspoon salt
¼ cup kasha (buckwheat groats), toasted
½ teaspoon sugar
3 tablespoons chilled stick margarine, cut into
    small pieces
¾ cup nonfat buttermilk
1 tablespoon all-purpose flour
Vegetable cooking spray

Combine first 6 ingredients in a large bowl; cut in margarine with a pastry blender until mixture resembles coarse meal. Add buttermilk; stir with a fork just until dry ingredients are moistened.

Sprinkle 1 tablespoon flour evenly over work surface. Turn dough out onto floured surface; knead 10 to 12 times. Roll dough to ½-inch thickness; cut into rounds with a 2-inch biscuit cutter. Place rounds on a baking sheet coated with cooking spray. Bake at 425° for 10 minutes or until golden. Yield: 16 biscuits.

PER BISCUIT: 79 CALORIES (26% FROM FAT)
FAT 2.3G (SATURATED FAT 0.5G)
PROTEIN 2.0G CARBOHYDRATE 12.5G
CHOLESTEROL 0MG SODIUM 169MG

PEPPERY BISCUITS

2 cups all-purpose flour
2 teaspoons baking powder
¼ teaspoon salt
1 to 1½ teaspoons coarsely ground pepper
½ teaspoon sugar
⅛ teaspoon garlic powder
3 tablespoons chilled stick margarine, cut into
    small pieces
¾ cup 1% low-fat milk or beer

Combine first 6 ingredients in a large bowl; cut in margarine with a pastry blender until mixture resembles coarse meal. Add milk, stirring just until dry ingredients are moistened.

Turn dough out onto a floured surface; knead 4 or 5 times. Roll dough to ½-inch thickness; cut into rounds with a 2½-inch biscuit cutter. Place rounds on a baking sheet. Bake at 450° for 11 minutes or until golden. Yield: 1 dozen.

PER BISCUIT: 109 CALORIES (26% FROM FAT)
FAT 3.2G (SATURATED FAT 0.7G)
PROTEIN 2.7G CARBOHYDRATE 17.1G
CHOLESTEROL 1MG SODIUM 140MG

SOUR CREAM AND CHIVE BISCUITS

(pictured on page 15)

2 cups all-purpose flour
1 tablespoon baking powder
¼ teaspoon salt
3 tablespoons minced fresh or freeze-dried
    chives
¾ cup skim milk
⅓ cup low-fat sour cream
2 tablespoons stick margarine, melted
Vegetable cooking spray

Combine first 4 ingredients in a large bowl. Combine milk, sour cream, and margarine; stir well. Add to flour mixture, stirring just until dry ingredients are moistened.

Drop batter by heaping tablespoonfuls onto a baking sheet coated with cooking spray. Bake at 450° for 11 minutes or until golden. Yield: 1 dozen.

PER BISCUIT: 109 CALORIES (25% FROM FAT)
FAT 3.0G (SATURATED FAT 0.9G)
PROTEIN 2.9G CARBOHYDRATE 17.2G
CHOLESTEROL 3MG SODIUM 157MG

Whole Wheat Yeast Biscuits

¼ cup warm water (105° to 115°)
1 package active dry yeast
1¾ cups plus 2 tablespoons all-purpose flour
¾ cup whole wheat flour
1 teaspoon baking powder
½ teaspoon baking soda
¼ teaspoon salt
1 tablespoon sugar
3 tablespoons chilled reduced-calorie stick
    margarine, cut into small pieces
⅔ cup nonfat buttermilk
2 tablespoons all-purpose flour
Vegetable cooking spray

Combine water and yeast; let mixture stand 5 minutes. Combine 1¾ cups plus 2 tablespoons all-purpose flour and next 5 ingredients in a large bowl; cut in margarine with a pastry blender until mixture resembles coarse meal. Add yeast mixture and buttermilk, stirring just until dry ingredients are moistened. Cover and chill 8 hours.

Sprinkle 2 tablespoons all-purpose flour evenly over work surface. Turn dough out onto floured surface, and knead 1 minute. Roll dough to ½-inch thickness; cut into rounds with a 2-inch biscuit cutter. Place rounds on a baking sheet coated with cooking spray. Bake at 425° for 10 to 12 minutes or until golden. Yield: 16 biscuits.

Per Biscuit: 82 Calories (19% from Fat)
Fat 1.7g (Saturated Fat 0.3g)
Protein 2.5g   Carbohydrate 14.5g
Cholesterol 0mg   Sodium 138mg

Whole Wheat Yeast Biscuits

RAISIN BISCUITS

1¾ cups all-purpose flour
2 teaspoons baking powder
¼ teaspoon salt
⅓ cup raisins
2 tablespoons sugar
1¼ teaspoons ground cinnamon
⅔ cup nonfat buttermilk
2 tablespoons vegetable oil
Vegetable cooking spray
½ cup sifted powdered sugar
1 tablespoon unsweetened apple juice

Combine first 6 ingredients in a large bowl; make a well in center of mixture. Combine buttermilk and oil; add to flour mixture, stirring just until dry ingredients are moistened. Turn out onto work surface; knead 4 or 5 times. Roll dough to ½-inch thickness; cut into rounds with a 2-inch biscuit cutter. Place rounds on a baking sheet coated with cooking spray. Bake at 425° for 10 minutes or until golden.

Combine powdered sugar and apple juice; stir well. Drizzle over warm biscuits. Yield: 1½ dozen.

PER BISCUIT: 89 CALORIES (17% FROM FAT)
FAT 1.7G (SATURATED FAT 0.3G)
PROTEIN 1.7G CARBOHYDRATE 16.9G
CHOLESTEROL 0MG SODIUM 87MG

Baker's Tip

Use dental floss or string to slice a roll of dough without flattening the sides. Slide the floss under the dough; slowly pull up the floss to cut through the roll. This works for the pinwheels on this page as well as Cinnamon Rolls and Lemon-Glazed Cranberry Rolls on page 51.

RED PEPPER-ROSEMARY PINWHEELS

Use dental floss as described at left to cut the roll of dough into even, round slices.

Vegetable cooking spray
½ cup finely chopped sweet red pepper
¼ cup minced onion
1 clove garlic, minced
1 tablespoon fresh rosemary, minced
¼ teaspoon ground red pepper
1¼ cups all-purpose flour
1 teaspoon baking powder
¼ teaspoon salt
3 tablespoons chilled reduced-calorie stick
    margarine, cut into small pieces
1 egg, lightly beaten
3 tablespoons skim milk

Coat a nonstick skillet with cooking spray; place over medium-high heat until hot. Add chopped red pepper, onion, and garlic; sauté until tender. Add rosemary and ground pepper; remove from heat, and set aside.

Combine flour, baking powder, and salt in a large bowl; cut in margarine with a pastry blender until mixture resembles coarse meal. Combine egg and milk; add to flour mixture, stirring just until dry ingredients are moistened. Turn dough out onto a lightly floured surface; knead 5 or 6 times.

Place dough between two pieces of heavy-duty plastic wrap; roll into a 10- x 8-inch rectangle. Remove top piece of plastic wrap. Spread vegetable mixture evenly over dough. Roll up, jellyroll fashion, starting at long side. Pinch ends and seam to seal.

Cut roll into 10 (1-inch) slices. Place slices in muffin pans coated with cooking spray. Bake at 400° for 15 to 18 minutes or until golden. Remove from pans immediately. Yield: 10 pinwheels.

PER PINWHEEL: 90 CALORIES (31% FROM FAT)
FAT 3.1G (SATURATED FAT 0.5G)
PROTEIN 2.6G CARBOHYDRATE 13.3G
CHOLESTEROL 22MG SODIUM 141MG

Red Pepper-Rosemary Pinwheels

CRANBERRY-ORANGE SCONES

1 cup all-purpose flour
1 cup sifted cake flour
2 teaspoons baking powder
½ teaspoon baking soda
¼ teaspoon salt
⅔ cup sugar
3 tablespoons chilled stick margarine, cut into small pieces
¾ cup fresh or frozen cranberries, thawed and halved
2 teaspoons grated orange rind
¾ cup plain nonfat yogurt
Vegetable cooking spray
2 teaspoons sugar

Combine first 6 ingredients in a large bowl; cut in margarine with a pastry blender until mixture resembles coarse meal. Add cranberries and orange rind; toss well. Add yogurt, stirring just until dry ingredients are moistened (dough will be sticky).

Turn dough out onto a lightly floured surface; knead 4 or 5 times, using floured hands. Pat dough into an 8-inch circle on a baking sheet coated with cooking spray. Cut dough into 12 wedges (do not separate wedges). Sprinkle 2 teaspoons sugar over dough. Bake at 450° for 12 minutes or until golden. Serve warm. Yield: 1 dozen.

PER SCONE: 147 CALORIES (19% FROM FAT)
FAT 3.1G (SATURATED FAT 0.6G)
PROTEIN 2.5G CARBOHYDRATE 27.4G
CHOLESTEROL 0MG SODIUM 195MG

STREUSEL-OAT SCONES

These hearty scones are best served warm.

2 cups all-purpose flour
2 teaspoons baking powder
¼ teaspoon baking soda
¼ teaspoon salt
¼ cup sugar
¼ cup chilled stick margarine, cut into small pieces
¾ cup low-fat buttermilk
Vegetable cooking spray
¼ cup quick-cooking oats, uncooked
¼ cup firmly packed brown sugar
1 tablespoon stick margarine, melted
1 tablespoon all-purpose flour

Combine first 5 ingredients in a large bowl; cut in ¼ cup margarine with a pastry blender until mixture resembles coarse meal. Add buttermilk, stirring just until dry ingredients are moistened. Turn dough out onto a baking sheet coated with cooking spray. Pat dough into an 8-inch circle.

Combine oats and remaining 3 ingredients. Gently pat oats mixture into surface of dough. Cut dough into 12 wedges (do not separate wedges). Bake at 450° for 15 minutes or until lightly browned. Serve warm. Yield: 1 dozen.

PER SCONE: 169 CALORIES (29% FROM FAT)
FAT 5.4G (SATURATED FAT 1.2G)
PROTEIN 3.1G CARBOHYDRATE 27.2G
CHOLESTEROL 0MG SODIUM 208MG

Steps to Success

Follow these tips for tender, flaky biscuits and scones.
• Cut margarine into dry ingredients thoroughly. A pastry blender is the tool of choice, although you can make do with two knives or a fork.
•After adding liquid to the dry ingredients, stir just until the dry ingredients are moistened.

Too much mixing makes biscuits tough and heavy.
• Knead the dough on a lightly floured surface just until the dough feels soft and not sticky.
• Cut the dough with a floured biscuit cutter to prevent the dough from sticking to the cutter.

STRAWBERRY-PECAN SCONES

(pictured on page 12)

2   cups all-purpose flour
2   teaspoons baking powder
½   teaspoon baking soda
¼   teaspoon salt
¼   cup sugar
3   tablespoons chilled stick margarine, cut into
      small pieces
1   (8-ounce) carton vanilla low-fat yogurt
Vegetable cooking spray
¼   cup no-sugar-added strawberry or
      raspberry spread
2   tablespoons finely chopped pecans

Combine first 5 ingredients in a large bowl; cut in margarine with a pastry blender until mixture resembles coarse meal. Add yogurt, stirring just until dry ingredients are moistened (dough will be sticky).

Turn dough out onto a lightly floured surface; knead 4 or 5 times, using floured hands. Pat dough into an 8-inch circle on a baking sheet coated with cooking spray. Cut dough into 12 wedges, cutting to, but not through, dough; make a small slit in center of each wedge. Place 1 teaspoon strawberry spread on each slit; sprinkle with pecans. Bake at 400° for 13 minutes or until golden. Serve warm. Yield: 1 dozen.

PER SCONE: 147 CALORIES (26% FROM FAT)
FAT 4.2G (SATURATED FAT 0.8G)
PROTEIN 3.1G   CARBOHYDRATE 24.2G
CHOLESTEROL 1MG   SODIUM 215MG

Pat dough into an 8-inch circle on a baking sheet coated with cooking spray.

Cut dough into 12 wedges, cutting to, but not through, dough.

Make a small slit in center of each wedge; place strawberry spread on top of each slit, and sprinkle with pecans.

Sun-Dried Tomato and Feta Scones

SUN-DRIED TOMATO AND FETA SCONES

¼ cup sun-dried tomato pieces (packed without oil)
1 cup boiling water
2 cups all-purpose flour
2 teaspoons baking powder
¼ teaspoon salt
1 teaspoon dried basil
2 tablespoons chilled stick margarine, cut into small pieces
¼ cup crumbled feta cheese
½ cup 1% low-fat milk
¼ teaspoon hot sauce
1 egg, lightly beaten
Vegetable cooking spray

Combine tomato and boiling water; let stand 10 minutes. Drain; press between paper towels.

Combine flour and next 3 ingredients in a large bowl; cut in margarine with a pastry blender until mixture resembles coarse meal. Combine tomato, feta cheese, and next 3 ingredients; add to flour mixture, stirring just until dry ingredients are moistened (dough will be sticky).

Pat dough to ½-inch thickness on a lightly floured surface, using floured hands. Cut into rounds with a 2½-inch biscuit cutter. Place rounds, 2 inches apart, on a baking sheet coated with cooking spray. Bake at 400° for 12 minutes or until golden. Serve warm. Yield: 1 dozen.

PER SCONE: 109 CALORIES (26% FROM FAT)
FAT 3.2G (SATURATED FAT 1.0G)
PROTEIN 3.4G CARBOHYDRATE 16.4G
CHOLESTEROL 20MG SODIUM 183MG

SAVORY CHEESE BISCOTTI

2 cups all-purpose flour
1 teaspoon baking powder
1 teaspoon salt
2 tablespoons yellow cornmeal
1 teaspoon sugar
½ teaspoon dried basil
3 egg whites, lightly beaten
½ cup nonfat sour cream
2 tablespoons stick margarine, melted
½ cup (2 ounces) shredded smoked Cheddar cheese
Vegetable cooking spray

Combine first 6 ingredients in a large bowl. Combine egg whites, sour cream, and margarine in a small bowl; stir with a wire whisk until blended. Stir in cheese; add to flour mixture, stirring until well blended (dough will be crumbly).

Turn dough out onto a lightly floured surface; knead 7 or 8 times. Shape dough into a 16-inch-long roll. Place roll on a baking sheet coated with cooking spray; flatten roll to 1-inch thickness.

Bake at 350° for 30 minutes. Remove roll from baking sheet to a wire rack; cool 10 minutes. Cut roll diagonally into 24 (½-inch) slices; place slices, cut sides down, on baking sheet. Reduce oven temperature to 325°; bake 15 minutes. Turn slices over; bake 15 minutes (biscotti will be slightly soft in center but will harden as they cool). Remove from baking sheet; cool on wire rack. Yield: 2 dozen.

PER BISCOTTO: 65 CALORIES (26% FROM FAT)
FAT 1.9G (SATURATED FAT 0.7G)
PROTEIN 2.5G CARBOHYDRATE 9.2G
CHOLESTEROL 2MG SODIUM 151MG

Clockwise from top left: *Spicy Cheese Crackers, Onion Bagel Thins, and Vegetable Crisps*

ONION BAGEL THINS

2 (3½-ounce) plain bagels
2 tablespoons reduced-calorie stick margarine, melted
½ teaspoon onion powder

Cut 1 bagel in half vertically, using an electric knife, to form 2 thick half-circles. Place each bagel half, cut side down, on a flat surface; cut each half into 8 slices. Repeat procedure with remaining bagel.

Place slices on a baking sheet. Combine margarine and onion powder; brush over bagels.

Bake at 325° for 20 minutes or until golden and crisp. Remove from pan; cool completely on wire racks. Store in an airtight container. Yield: 32 crackers.

PER CRACKER: 21 CALORIES (26% FROM FAT)
FAT 0.6G (SATURATED FAT 0.1G)
PROTEIN 0.7G CARBOHYDRATE 3.3G
CHOLESTEROL 0MG SODIUM 40MG

SPICY CHEESE CRACKERS

1 cup all-purpose flour
¼ teaspoon baking soda
½ teaspoon salt
½ cup yellow cornmeal
¼ teaspoon ground red pepper
⅛ teaspoon ground cumin
2 tablespoons shredded reduced-fat Cheddar cheese
½ cup nonfat buttermilk
2 tablespoons vegetable oil
Vegetable cooking spray

Combine first 6 ingredients; stir in cheese. Add buttermilk and oil; stir just until dry ingredients are moistened.

Divide dough in half, shaping each half into a ball. Roll 1 ball into an 11- x 9-inch paper-thin rectangle on a baking sheet coated with cooking spray. Score dough by making 8 lengthwise cuts and 10 crosswise cuts. Prick surface with a fork.

Bake at 350° for 20 minutes or until crisp and lightly browned. Remove from pans; cool on wire racks. Separate into crackers. Repeat procedure. Store in an airtight container. Yield: 16½ dozen.

PER CRACKER: 5 CALORIES (36% FROM FAT)
FAT 0.2G (SATURATED FAT 0.0G)
PROTEIN 0.1G CARBOHYDRATE 0.8G
CHOLESTEROL 0MG SODIUM 9MG

VEGETABLE CRISPS

3 tablespoons dried sweet red or green pepper flakes
2 tablespoons dried celery flakes
1 teaspoon dried crushed red pepper
1½ cups all-purpose flour
½ cup whole wheat flour
2 tablespoons sugar
1 teaspoon dried oregano
½ teaspoon baking soda
½ teaspoon salt
½ teaspoon chicken-flavored bouillon granules
¼ cup shortening
½ cup warm water
Vegetable cooking spray

Position knife blade in food processor bowl; add first 3 ingredients. Process 15 seconds. Add all-purpose flour and next 8 ingredients; process until dough leaves sides of bowl and forms a ball. Divide dough in half, shaping each half into a ball; cover and let rest 10 minutes.

Roll 1 portion into a 13½- x 12-inch paper-thin rectangle on a baking sheet coated with cooking spray. Score dough by making 7 lengthwise cuts and 8 crosswise cuts. Prick entire surface of dough liberally with a fork.

Bake at 350° for 15 minutes or until crisp. Remove from pans; cool on wire racks. Separate into crackers. Repeat with remaining dough. Store in an airtight container. Yield: 12 dozen.

PER CRACKER: 10 CALORIES (27% FROM FAT)
FAT 0.3G (SATURATED FAT 0.1G)
PROTEIN 0.2G CARBOHYDRATE 1.6G
CHOLESTEROL 0MG SODIUM 16MG

Banana Muffins (recipe on page 32)

QUICK MUFFINS & LOAVES

*B*ake a batch of Apple-Pecan Muffins (page 32) to serve with orange juice, and you've got breakfast. Harvest Corn Muffins (page 28) will transform a simple bowl of chili into a satisfying lunch or supper. And when you prepare Banana Muffins (page 32), your children can enjoy a healthy, delicious snack any time.

The point, of course, is that muffins are versatile. And—like biscuits and scones—they're quick. This chapter presents a variety of savory and sweet muffins, popovers, cornbreads, and loaf breads. All are classified as quick breads because their batters are prepared and then baked immediately—ready for your enjoyment.

Harvest Corn Muffins

HARVEST CORN MUFFINS

1 cup all-purpose flour
1 tablespoon plus 1 teaspoon baking powder
¼ teaspoon salt
1 cup cornmeal
2 tablespoons brown sugar
½ teaspoon dried oregano
¼ teaspoon ground white pepper
1 cup skim milk
1 cup cooked, mashed or canned pumpkin
3 tablespoons diced pimiento
2 tablespoons vegetable oil
1 egg, lightly beaten
2 egg whites, lightly beaten
1 jalapeño pepper, seeded and minced
Vegetable cooking spray
½ cup (2 ounces) finely shredded reduced-fat
    Cheddar cheese

Combine first 7 ingredients in a large bowl; make a well in center of mixture. Combine milk and next 6 ingredients; add to flour mixture, stirring just until dry ingredients are moistened.

Spoon batter into muffin pans coated with cooking spray, filling two-thirds full. Sprinkle cheese evenly over batter. Bake at 400° for 20 minutes or until lightly browned. Remove muffins from pans immediately. Yield: 1½ dozen.

PER MUFFIN: 98 CALORIES (27% FROM FAT)
FAT 2.9G (SATURATED FAT 0.8G)
PROTEIN 3.7G CARBOHYDRATE 14.3G
CHOLESTEROL 15MG SODIUM 163MG

CHILE CORN STICKS

1½ teaspoons vegetable oil
½ cup diced sweet red pepper
⅓ cup seeded, diced Anaheim chile
¼ cup diced onion
1 clove garlic, minced
¾ cup all-purpose flour
2 teaspoons baking powder
¼ teaspoon baking soda
¼ teaspoon salt
¾ cup yellow cornmeal
1½ tablespoons sugar
¾ cup corn cut from cob (about 1½ ears)
1 egg, lightly beaten
1 cup nonfat buttermilk
Vegetable cooking spray

Heat oil in a skillet over medium heat. Add red pepper and next 3 ingredients; sauté 5 minutes.

Combine flour and next 5 ingredients in a medium bowl. Add red pepper mixture and corn; stir well. Make a well in center of mixture. Combine egg and buttermilk; add to flour mixture, stirring just until dry ingredients are moistened.

Coat cast-iron corn stick pans heavily with cooking spray; place in a 400° oven 10 minutes. Spoon batter evenly into preheated pans. Bake at 400° for 20 minutes or until lightly browned. Remove corn sticks from pans immediately, and serve warm. Yield: 14 corn sticks.

PER CORN STICK: 87 CALORIES (16% FROM FAT)
FAT 1.5G (SATURATED FAT 0.3G)
PROTEIN 2.8G CARBOHYDRATE 16.0G
CHOLESTEROL 16MG SODIUM 139MG

COWBOY CORNBREAD

1 tablespoon plus 1 teaspoon vegetable oil, divided
¾ cup all-purpose flour
1½ teaspoons baking powder
¼ teaspoon baking soda
¼ teaspoon salt
1 cup yellow cornmeal
1 egg, lightly beaten
¾ cup low-fat buttermilk
1 (4.5-ounce) can chopped green chiles, undrained
1 cup frozen whole-kernel corn, thawed
10 sweet red pepper strips

Coat an 8-inch cast-iron skillet with 1 teaspoon oil. Place in a 400° oven 10 minutes.

Combine flour and next 4 ingredients in a large bowl. Combine remaining 1 tablespoon oil, egg, buttermilk, and chiles; add to cornmeal mixture, stirring just until dry ingredients are moistened. Stir in corn.

Spoon batter into preheated skillet. Arrange pepper strips over batter. Bake at 400° for 45 minutes or until a wooden pick inserted in center comes out clean. To serve, cut into wedges. Yield: 10 wedges.

PER WEDGE: 138 CALORIES (20% FROM FAT)
FAT 3.0G (SATURATED FAT 0.5G)
PROTEIN 4.3G CARBOHYDRATE 23.9G
CHOLESTEROL 22MG SODIUM 189MG

All about Cornmeal

Cornbread is a type of quick bread that substitutes cornmeal for most, if not all, of the flour. Cornmeal comes in either plain or self-rising form and is ground from white, yellow, or blue corn. You can use all three colors of cornmeal interchangeably in recipes, although white cornmeal is milder tasting than the other two. Unlike regular ground cornmeal, stone-ground cornmeal produces cornbread with a coarse, slightly crunchy texture.

You can buy cornmeal plain or in the convenient self-rising or mix forms.

BROCCOLI CORNBREAD

1 tablespoon reduced-calorie stick
   margarine
Vegetable cooking spray
½ (10-ounce) package frozen chopped
   broccoli, thawed and drained
1 (8½-ounce) package corn muffin mix
¾ cup 1% low-fat cottage cheese
½ cup fat-free egg substitute
½ cup finely chopped onion
1 (2-ounce) jar diced pimiento, drained
¼ teaspoon cracked pepper

Place margarine in an 8-inch square pan coated with cooking spray. Place pan in a 350° oven for 3 minutes or until margarine melts. Tilt pan to coat bottom with margarine; set aside.

Press broccoli between paper towels to remove excess moisture. Combine broccoli, muffin mix, and remaining 5 ingredients in a bowl, stirring mixture well.

Spoon batter into prepared pan. Bake at 350° for 1 hour or until golden. To serve, cut into squares. Yield: 16 squares.

PER SQUARE: 82 CALORIES (24% FROM FAT)
FAT 2.2G (SATURATED FAT 0.7G)
PROTEIN 3.4G   CARBOHYDRATE 12.2G
CHOLESTEROL 0MG   SODIUM 186MG

Broccoli Cornbread

POPOVERS

1⅓ cups all-purpose flour
2 teaspoons sugar
¼ teaspoon salt
1 cup 2% low-fat milk
1 egg
2 egg whites
Vegetable cooking spray

Combine first 3 ingredients; set aside. Combine milk, egg, and egg whites in a glass measure or bowl, stirring with a wire whisk until blended. Gradually add flour mixture, stirring with whisk.

Heat popover pans at 450° for 3 minutes; remove from oven, and coat with cooking spray. Spoon batter into popover pan cups, filling half full. Bake at 450° for 10 minutes; reduce heat to 350°, and bake 25 minutes or until golden. Remove from pans. Serve immediately. Yield: 8 popovers.

PER POPOVER: 111 CALORIES (14% FROM FAT)
FAT 1.7G (SATURATED FAT 0.6G)
PROTEIN 4.8G CARBOHYDRATE 18.5G
CHOLESTEROL 30MG SODIUM 110MG

HERB POPOVERS

Prepare Popovers, adding 1 teaspoon rubbed sage or ½ teaspoon dried dillweed with flour mixture. Yield: 8 popovers.

PER POPOVER: 111 CALORIES (14% FROM FAT)
FAT 1.7G (SATURATED FAT 0.6G)
PROTEIN 4.8G CARBOHYDRATE 18.5G
CHOLESTEROL 30MG SODIUM 110MG

Baker's Tip

Although baking popovers in a popover pan produces taller, airier popovers, you can use muffin pans. Just spoon the batter evenly into eight heated cups. Bake at 450° for 10 minutes; then lower the temperature to 350° (do not remove pans from the oven). Bake 15 additional minutes or until popovers are puffed and golden.

Combine flour, sugar, and salt. Combine milk, egg, and egg whites in a large bowl, stirring with a wire whisk. Gradually add flour mixture to milk mixture, stirring with whisk.

Pour batter evenly into eight heated popover cups, filling each cup half full; add water to any empty cups to prevent scorching.

Bake until puffed and golden. Remove popovers from pan, and serve immediately.

APPLE-PECAN MUFFINS

Crusty, swirled tops form as the muffins bake.

1½ cups all-purpose flour
1¼ teaspoons baking soda
¼ teaspoon salt
1 cup wheat bran flakes cereal with raisins
⅔ cup sugar
⅓ cup graham cracker crumbs
1 egg, lightly beaten
1 cup nonfat buttermilk
2 tablespoons stick margarine, melted
1 cup peeled, finely chopped Rome apple
⅓ cup chopped pecans, toasted
2 tablespoons sugar
¾ teaspoon ground cinnamon
1 tablespoon stick margarine, melted
Vegetable cooking spray
1 tablespoon sugar

Combine first 6 ingredients in a large bowl; make a well in center of mixture. Combine egg, butter-milk, and 2 tablespoons margarine; add to flour mixture, stirring just until dry ingredients are moistened.

Combine apple and next 4 ingredients. Spoon 2 tablespoons batter into each of 12 muffin pans coated with cooking spray. Top evenly with apple mixture; spoon remaining batter over apple mixture. (Batter will not cover apple mixture completely.) Sprinkle 1 tablespoon sugar evenly over batter. Bake at 350° for 25 minutes. Remove from pans immediately. Yield: 1 dozen.

PER MUFFIN: 198 CALORIES (28% FROM FAT)
FAT 6.1G (SATURATED FAT 0.9G)
PROTEIN 3.6G CARBOHYDRATE 33.4G
CHOLESTEROL 18MG SODIUM 240MG

BANANA MUFFINS

(pictured on page 26)

1⅓ cups all-purpose flour
⅔ cup whole wheat flour
1 teaspoon baking powder
1 teaspoon baking soda
½ teaspoon salt
⅔ cup sugar
1¼ cups mashed ripe banana (about 3 large)
¼ cup vegetable oil
1 egg, lightly beaten
Vegetable cooking spray

Combine first 6 ingredients; make a well in the center of mixture. Combine banana, oil, and egg; add to flour mixture, stirring just until dry ingredients are moistened. Spoon batter into muffin pans coated with cooking spray, filling two-thirds full. Bake at 400° for 15 minutes or until golden. Remove from pans immediately. Yield: 16 muffins.

PER MUFFIN: 136 CALORIES (28% FROM FAT)
FAT 4.2G (SATURATED FAT 0.8G)
PROTEIN 2.2G CARBOHYDRATE 23.2G
CHOLESTEROL 13MG SODIUM 154MG

Steps to Success

The secret to perfect muffins is in the stirring. Follow these tips:

• First, combine dry ingredients, and make a well in the center of the mixture.

• Combine liquid ingredients, such as milk, margarine, and egg; stir well.

• Add liquid ingredients to flour mixture. (See page 40 for a photo of this technique.) Stir only until dry ingredients are moistened. The batter will be lumpy.

• If baked muffins have pointed tops and tunnels throughout, you stirred too much. Stir less next time.

• Unless stated otherwise, remove muffins from pans immediately after baking to prevent them from getting moist on the bottom.

BLUEBERRY-OAT STREUSEL MUFFINS

(pictured on cover)

⅓ cup regular oats, uncooked
3 tablespoons brown sugar
1 tablespoon all-purpose flour
1 tablespoon reduced-calorie stick margarine
2 tablespoons chopped almonds
2 cups all-purpose flour
2 teaspoons baking powder
¼ teaspoon baking soda
¼ teaspoon salt
½ cup sugar
2 teaspoons grated lemon rind
1½ cups fresh or frozen blueberries, thawed
    and drained
1 egg, lightly beaten
¾ cup nonfat buttermilk
¼ cup vegetable oil
Vegetable cooking spray

Position knife blade in food processor bowl. Add first 3 ingredients; process 5 seconds or until mixture resembles fine meal. Add margarine, and pulse 5 times or until mixture resembles coarse meal. Transfer to a small bowl, and stir in almonds; set oats mixture aside.

Combine 2 cups flour and next 5 ingredients in a large bowl. Add blueberries; toss gently to combine. Make a well in center of mixture. Combine egg, buttermilk, and oil; add to flour mixture, stirring just until dry ingredients are moistened.

Spoon batter into muffin pans coated with cooking spray, filling two-thirds full. Sprinkle evenly with oats mixture. Bake at 400° for 15 to 20 minutes or until golden. Remove muffins from pans immediately. Yield: 14 muffins.

PER MUFFIN: 177 CALORIES (31% FROM FAT)
FAT 6.0G (SATURATED FAT 1.1G)
PROTEIN 3.5G CARBOHYDRATE 27.9G
CHOLESTEROL 16MG SODIUM 185MG

CHERRY MUFFINS

1 cup dried sweet cherries
½ cup unsweetened apple juice
1¾ cups all-purpose flour
2½ teaspoons baking powder
¼ teaspoon salt
½ cup sugar
1 teaspoon grated lemon rind
½ cup plus 2 tablespoons skim milk
2 tablespoons vegetable oil
1 teaspoon almond extract
1 egg, lightly beaten
Vegetable cooking spray
2 teaspoons sugar

Combine cherries and apple juice; let stand 30 minutes. Drain, reserving ¼ cup juice. Coarsely chop cherries.

Combine flour and next 4 ingredients; make a well in center of mixture. Combine reserved juice, milk, and next 3 ingredients. Add to flour mixture, stirring just until dry ingredients are moistened. Fold in cherries.

Spoon batter into muffin pans coated with cooking spray, filling two-thirds full; sprinkle 2 teaspoons sugar evenly over batter. Bake at 400° for 15 to 18 minutes or until golden. Remove from pans immediately. Yield: 15 muffins.

PER MUFFIN: 138 CALORIES (19% FROM FAT)
FAT 2.9G (SATURATED FAT 0.6G)
PROTEIN 2.7G CARBOHYDRATE 25.7G
CHOLESTEROL 15MG SODIUM 116MG

TRIPLE-LEMON MUFFINS

2 cups all-purpose flour
1 teaspoon baking powder
½ teaspoon baking soda
¼ teaspoon salt
½ cup sugar
2 eggs, lightly beaten
3 tablespoons stick margarine, melted
1 teaspoon grated lemon rind
2 tablespoons fresh lemon juice
1 (8-ounce) carton lemon low-fat yogurt
Vegetable cooking spray
2 tablespoons fresh lemon juice
1½ tablespoons sugar

Combine first 5 ingredients in a large bowl; make a well in center of mixture. Combine eggs and next 4 ingredients, stirring well with a wire whisk; add to flour mixture, stirring just until dry ingredients are moistened.

Spoon batter into muffin pans coated with cooking spray. Bake at 400° for 20 minutes or until golden.

Combine 2 tablespoons lemon juice and 1½ tablespoons sugar in a small saucepan; bring to a boil. Cook 2 minutes or until slightly thickened. Brush hot muffins with lemon glaze; remove muffins from pans immediately. Yield: 1 dozen.

PER MUFFIN: 181 CALORIES (21% FROM FAT)
FAT 4.3G (SATURATED FAT 0.9G)
PROTEIN 4.0G CARBOHYDRATE 4.3G
CHOLESTEROL 37MG SODIUM 175MG

ORANGE GINGERBREAD MUFFINS

2 cups reduced-fat biscuit and baking mix
¼ cup cinnamon sugar, divided
½ teaspoon ground ginger
1 egg, lightly beaten
⅔ cup skim milk
¼ cup molasses
1 tablespoon grated orange rind
Butter-flavored vegetable cooking spray

Combine baking mix, 3½ tablespoons cinnamon sugar, and ginger in a large bowl; make a well in center of mixture. Combine egg and next 3 ingredients, stirring well; add to dry ingredients, stirring just until dry ingredients are moistened.

Spoon batter into muffin pans coated with cooking spray, filling half full; sprinkle remaining 1½ teaspoons cinnamon sugar evenly over batter. Bake at 400° for 12 minutes. Remove from pans immediately. Yield: 1 dozen.

Note: To make your own cinnamon sugar, combine ¼ cup sugar and 1½ teaspoons ground cinnamon.

PER MUFFIN: 122 CALORIES (15% FROM FAT)
FAT 2.0G (SATURATED FAT 0.4G)
PROTEIN 2.5G CARBOHYDRATE 24.0G
CHOLESTEROL 19MG SODIUM 247MG

PUMPKIN-OAT BRAN MUFFINS

½ cup all-purpose flour
2 teaspoons baking powder
¼ teaspoon salt
1½ cups oat bran
⅔ cup firmly packed brown sugar
1 teaspoon pumpkin pie spice
1 cup cooked, mashed or canned pumpkin
½ cup skim milk
2 tablespoons vegetable oil
2 egg whites, lightly beaten
Vegetable cooking spray

Combine first 6 ingredients in a large bowl. Make a well in center of mixture. Combine pumpkin and next 3 ingredients; stir well. Add pumpkin mixture to flour mixture, stirring just until dry ingredients are moistened.

Spoon batter into muffin pans coated with cooking spray, filling two-thirds full. Bake at 425° for 20 minutes. Remove from pans immediately. Serve with light syrup, if desired. Yield: 1 dozen.

PER MUFFIN: 136 CALORIES (23% FROM FAT)
FAT 3.4G (SATURATED FAT 0.5G)
PROTEIN 3.6G CARBOHYDRATE 23.5G
CHOLESTEROL 0MG SODIUM 135MG

Pumpkin-Oat Bran Muffins

PEAR-OATMEAL MUFFINS

Ricotta cheese acts as a tenderizer when worked into this muffin batter. The rich yet subtle taste of the cheese doesn't overwhelm other flavors.

2½ cups all-purpose flour
1 tablespoon baking powder
1 teaspoon baking soda
½ teaspoon salt
¾ cup sugar
½ cup quick-cooking oats, uncooked
¼ teaspoon ground cardamom
¼ teaspoon ground allspice
2 cups chopped ripe pear
1 egg
1 egg white
¾ cup nonfat buttermilk
⅓ cup part-skim ricotta cheese
¼ cup vegetable oil
1 tablespoon vanilla extract
Vegetable cooking spray
½ cup quick-cooking oats, uncooked

Combine first 8 ingredients in a large bowl. Stir in pear; make a well in center of mixture. Combine egg and next 5 ingredients, stirring well with a whisk; add to flour mixture, stirring just until dry ingredients are moistened.

Spoon batter into muffin pans coated with cooking spray; sprinkle ½ cup oats evenly over batter. Bake at 400° for 18 minutes or until done. Remove from pans immediately. Yield: 1½ dozen.

PER MUFFIN: 165 CALORIES (24% FROM FAT)
FAT 4.4G (SATURATED FAT 1.0G)
PROTEIN 3.9G CARBOHYDRATE 27.3G
CHOLESTEROL 14MG SODIUM 157MG

PINEAPPLE-CARROT MUFFINS

If you've given up nuts because of the fat content, you can still enjoy nutty flavor by using whole wheat flour, which is made from entire grains of wheat.

1 (8-ounce) can crushed pineapple in juice, undrained
1 cup all-purpose flour
1 cup whole wheat flour
1 tablespoon baking powder
½ teaspoon baking soda
¼ teaspoon salt
½ cup firmly packed brown sugar
1 cup skim milk
½ cup fat-free egg substitute
¼ cup unsweetened applesauce
2 tablespoons vegetable oil
1 cup finely shredded carrot
½ cup golden raisins
Vegetable cooking spray

Drain pineapple, reserving juice for another use. Press pineapple between paper towels to remove excess moisture; set aside.

Combine all-purpose flour and next 5 ingredients in a large bowl; make a well in center of mixture. Combine milk and next 3 ingredients; add to flour mixture, stirring just until dry ingredients are moistened. Stir in pineapple, carrot, and raisins.

Spoon batter into muffin pans coated with cooking spray, filling three-fourths full. Bake at 400° for 20 to 22 minutes or until golden. Remove from pans immediately. Yield: 1½ dozen.

PER MUFFIN: 113 CALORIES (16% FROM FAT)
FAT 2.0G (SATURATED FAT 0.4G)
PROTEIN 3.0G CARBOHYDRATE 21.9G
CHOLESTEROL 0MG SODIUM 157MG

Fresh Strawberry Muffins

FRESH STRAWBERRY MUFFINS

2½ cups all-purpose flour
1 teaspoon baking soda
½ teaspoon salt
⅔ cup sugar
¾ teaspoon ground cinnamon
1½ cups sliced fresh strawberries
1 egg, lightly beaten
1 egg white, lightly beaten
1 cup nonfat buttermilk
⅓ cup stick margarine, melted
1¼ teaspoons vanilla extract
Vegetable cooking spray
1½ tablespoons sugar

Combine first 5 ingredients. Add strawberries; stir well. Make a well in center of mixture. Combine egg and next 4 ingredients; add to flour mixture, stirring just until dry ingredients are moistened.

Spoon batter into muffin pans coated with cooking spray; sprinkle 1½ tablespoons sugar evenly over batter. Bake at 350° for 25 minutes or until a wooden pick inserted in center comes out clean. Remove from pans immediately Yield: 1½ dozen.

PER MUFFIN: 142 CALORIES (26% FROM FAT)
FAT 4.1G (SATURATED FAT 0.8G)
PROTEIN 2.9G CARBOHYDRATE 23.5G
CHOLESTEROL 13MG SODIUM 170MG

JAMAICAN BANANA BREAD

*Use very ripe bananas in this delicious
loaf bread—they're easier to mash and have a
sweeter, more intense flavor.*

2 tablespoons stick margarine,
    softened
2 tablespoons tub-style light cream
    cheese, softened
1 cup sugar
1 egg
2 cups all-purpose flour
2 teaspoons baking powder
½ teaspoon baking soda
⅛ teaspoon salt
1 cup mashed ripe banana
½ cup skim milk
2 tablespoons dark rum or ¼ teaspoon
    imitation rum extract
½ teaspoon grated lime rind
1 tablespoon plus 1 teaspoon lime juice,
    divided
1 teaspoon vanilla extract
¼ cup plus 2 tablespoons chopped pecans,
    toasted and divided
¼ cup plus 2 tablespoons flaked sweetened
    coconut, divided
Vegetable cooking spray
¼ cup firmly packed brown sugar
2 teaspoons margarine
2 teaspoons dark rum or ⅛ teaspoon
    imitation rum extract

Beat 2 tablespoons margarine and cream cheese
at medium speed of an electric mixer; add 1 cup
sugar, beating well. Add egg; beat well.

Combine flour and next 3 ingredients. Combine
banana, milk, 2 tablespoons rum, lime rind, 2 teaspoons lime juice, and vanilla; stir well. Add flour
mixture to margarine mixture alternately with
banana mixture, beginning and ending with flour
mixture; beat after each addition. Stir in ¼ cup
pecans and ¼ cup coconut.

Pour batter into an 8½- x 4½- x 3-inch loafpan
coated with cooking spray. Bake at 375° for 1 hour.

Cool in pan 10 minutes; remove from pan. Cool
slightly on a wire rack.

Combine brown sugar, 2 teaspoons margarine,
remaining 2 teaspoons lime juice, and 2 teaspoons
rum in a saucepan; bring to a simmer. Cook, stirring constantly, 1 minute. Remove from heat. Stir
in remaining 2 tablespoons pecans and remaining 2
tablespoons coconut; spoon mixture over loaf.
Yield: 1 loaf, 16 (½-inch) slices.

PER SLICE: 187 CALORIES (26% FROM FAT)
FAT 5.4G (SATURATED FAT 1.5G)
PROTEIN 2.9G   CARBOHYDRATE 32.2G
CHOLESTEROL 15MG   SODIUM 155MG

Jamaican Banana Bread

Date-Walnut Bread

DATE-WALNUT BREAD

Storing this sweet bread in foil before serving makes it more moist.

1 cup chopped pitted dates
⅓ cup chopped walnuts
1 cup boiling water
1 tablespoon stick margarine, softened
¾ cup sugar
1 egg
1½ cups all-purpose flour
1 teaspoon baking soda
¼ teaspoon salt
1 teaspoon vanilla extract
Vegetable cooking spray

Combine first 3 ingredients in a small bowl. Cover and let stand 30 minutes.

Beat margarine at medium speed of an electric mixer until creamy; gradually add sugar, beating well. Add egg; beat well. Combine flour, baking soda, and salt; add to margarine mixture, beating well (mixture will be crumbly). Add date mixture and vanilla, stirring well.

Pour batter into an 8½- x 4½- x 3-inch loafpan coated with cooking spray. Bake at 350° for 1 hour or until a wooden pick inserted in center comes out clean. Cool in pan 15 minutes. Remove bread from pan, and cool completely on a wire rack. Wrap bread in aluminum foil; let stand at least 8 hours. To serve, cut into slices. Serve with nonfat cream cheese, if desired. Yield: 1 loaf, 16 (½-inch) slices.

PER SLICE: 128 CALORIES (18% FROM FAT)
FAT 2.5G (SATURATED FAT 0.4G)
PROTEIN 2.3G   CARBOHYDRATE 24.8G
CHOLESTEROL 14MG   SODIUM 128MG

ZUCCHINI BREAD

2 cups coarsely shredded zucchini
3 cups all-purpose flour
1 teaspoon baking soda
¼ teaspoon baking powder
1 teaspoon salt
1¾ cups sugar
1 teaspoon ground cinnamon
¾ cup unsweetened applesauce
½ cup fat-free egg substitute
⅓ cup vegetable oil
1 tablespoon vanilla extract
Vegetable cooking spray

Place zucchini on several layers of paper towels, and cover with additional paper towels. Let stand 5 minutes, pressing down occasionally.

Combine flour and next 5 ingredients in a large bowl; make a well in center of mixture. Combine zucchini, applesauce, and next 3 ingredients; add to flour mixture, stirring just until dry ingredients are moistened.

Spoon batter into two 7½- x 3- x 2-inch loafpans coated with cooking spray. Bake at 350° for 1 hour and 15 minutes or until a wooden pick inserted in center comes out clean. Cool in pans on a wire rack 10 minutes. Remove from pans; cool completely on wire rack. Yield: 2 loaves, 14 (½-inch) slices each.

PER SLICE: 128 CALORIES (20% FROM FAT)
FAT 2.8G (SATURATED FAT 0.5G)
PROTEIN 1.9G   CARBOHYDRATE 23.9G
CHOLESTEROL 0MG   SODIUM 140MG

HUCKLEBERRY COFFEE CAKE

¼ cup stick margarine, softened
½ (8-ounce) package nonfat cream cheese
1 cup sugar
1 egg
1 cup all-purpose flour
1 teaspoon baking powder
¼ teaspoon salt
1 teaspoon vanilla extract
2 cups fresh or frozen huckleberries or
    blueberries, unthawed
Vegetable cooking spray
2 tablespoons sugar
1 teaspoon ground cinnamon

Beat margarine and cream cheese at medium speed of an electric mixer until creamy; gradually add 1 cup sugar, beating well. Add egg; beat well.

Combine flour, baking powder, and salt; stir into margarine mixture. Stir in vanilla; fold in berries. Pour batter into a 9-inch round cakepan coated with cooking spray. Combine 2 tablespoons sugar and cinnamon; sprinkle over batter. Bake at 350° for 1 hour; cool on a wire rack. To serve, cut into wedges. Yield: 10 wedges.

PER WEDGE: 209 CALORIES (23% FROM FAT)
FAT 5.3G (SATURATED FAT 1.0G)
PROTEIN 3.7G   CARBOHYDRATE 36.9G
CHOLESTEROL 24MG   SODIUM 228MG

Baker's Tip

When making quick breads such as muffins and loaf breads, it's important to use the right mixing techniques. Many recipes call for making a well in the center of combined dry ingredients. Once you add the combined liquid ingredients, keep stirring to a minimum—just until dry ingredients are moistened.

A few muffins and quick loaf breads call for beating with an electric mixer. These breads usually contain more sugar than traditional muffins and have a cakelike texture. Use a mixer only when the recipe calls for it.

Raspberry-Almond Coffee Cake

RASPBERRY-ALMOND COFFEE CAKE

1 cup fresh raspberries
3 tablespoons brown sugar
1 cup all-purpose flour
½ teaspoon baking powder
¼ teaspoon baking soda
⅛ teaspoon salt
⅓ cup sugar
1 egg, lightly beaten
½ cup plain low-fat yogurt
2 tablespoons stick margarine, melted
1 teaspoon vanilla extract
Vegetable cooking spray
1 tablespoon sliced almonds
¼ cup sifted powdered sugar
1 teaspoon skim milk
¼ teaspoon vanilla extract
Fresh raspberries (optional)

Combine raspberries and brown sugar in a small bowl; set aside.

Combine flour and next 4 ingredients in a large bowl. Combine egg and next 3 ingredients, stirring well; add to flour mixture, stirring just until dry ingredients are moistened.

Spoon two-thirds of batter into an 8-inch round cakepan coated with cooking spray; spread evenly. Top with raspberry mixture. Spoon remaining batter over raspberry mixture; top with almonds.

Bake at 350° for 40 minutes or until a wooden pick inserted in center comes out clean. Cool in pan on a wire rack 10 minutes.

Combine powdered sugar, milk, and ¼ teaspoon vanilla; stir well. Drizzle over cake. To serve, cut into wedges. Serve warm or at room temperature. Garnish with raspberries, if desired. Yield: 8 wedges.

PER WEDGE: 176 CALORIES (23% FROM FAT)
FAT 4.5G (SATURATED FAT 1.0G)
PROTEIN 3.5G CARBOHYDRATE 30.4G
CHOLESTEROL 28MG SODIUM 156MG

Refrigerator Yeast Rolls (recipe on page 44)

ROLLS, BAGELS & STICKS

*Y*east may come in a tiny package, but when combined with flour, water, and a few other ingredients, it works magic. This chapter and the one following are dedicated to a wide variety of breads leavened by yeast. Here you'll find basic rolls, rolls made with cheese, and rolls flavored with basil, dillweed, and green chiles. Also included is a recipe for Tender Yeast Rolls (page 44) that calls for the roll dough to be prepared in a bread machine.

Near the end of the chapter are recipes for bagels, breadsticks, and pretzels. Complete step-by-step directions and several how-to photographs take the mystique out of preparing these specialty yeast breads. But before you start baking bagels or yeast rolls of any kind, turn to page 9 for directions on working with yeast.

REFRIGERATOR YEAST ROLLS

(pictured on page 42)

Make this dough on the weekend, and you can have fresh homemade rolls throughout the week.

¼ cup warm water (105° to 115°)
1 package active dry yeast
1 teaspoon sugar
1¾ cups skim milk
⅓ cup plus 1 teaspoon sugar
¼ cup vegetable oil
1½ teaspoons salt
6 cups plus 1 tablespoon bread flour, divided
Butter-flavored vegetable cooking spray

Combine first 3 ingredients in a 1-cup liquid measuring cup; let stand 5 minutes.

Combine milk and next 3 ingredients in a small saucepan; cook over medium heat until sugar dissolves, stirring occasionally. Cool to 115°. Add yeast mixture to milk mixture, stirring well with a wire whisk.

Place 6 cups flour in a large bowl. Gradually add yeast mixture to flour, stirring to make a stiff dough. Place in a large bowl coated with cooking spray, turning to coat top. Let stand at room temperature 10 minutes. Cover; chill at least 8 hours. (Dough may remain in refrigerator up to 5 days.)

To make rolls, sprinkle remaining 1 tablespoon flour over work surface. Punch dough down; turn out onto floured surface, and knead 2 or 3 times. Divide dough into thirds. Working with 1 portion at a time, shape each portion of dough into 12 balls. Place balls in a 9-inch round cakepan coated with cooking spray. Repeat procedure with remaining portions of dough.

Cover and let rise in a warm place (85°), free from drafts, 45 minutes or until doubled in bulk. Bake at 400° for 10 to 12 minutes or until golden. Coat rolls lightly with cooking spray. Yield: 3 dozen.

PER ROLL: 110 CALORIES (16% FROM FAT)
FAT 2.0G (SATURATED FAT 0.3G)
PROTEIN 3.2G   CARBOHYDRATE 19.4G
CHOLESTEROL 0MG   SODIUM 104MG

TENDER YEAST ROLLS

4 cups bread flour
1 cup water
¼ cup plus 2 tablespoons sugar
3 tablespoons vegetable oil
1¼ teaspoons salt
1 egg, lightly beaten
1 package active dry yeast
Vegetable cooking spray

Follow manufacturer's instructions for placing first 7 ingredients into bread machine. Select dough cycle; start bread machine. After dough cycle is complete, remove dough from machine (do not bake). Turn dough out onto a lightly floured surface, and knead 30 seconds. Cover dough, and let rest 10 minutes. Punch dough down, and divide into 18 equal portions.

Shape each portion into a ball; place on baking sheets coated with cooking spray. Cover and let rise in a warm place (85°), free from drafts, 20 minutes. Uncover and bake at 400° for 13 minutes or until browned. Yield: 1½ dozen.

PER ROLL: 152 CALORIES (18% FROM FAT)
FAT 3.1G (SATURATED FAT 0.6G)
PROTEIN 4.1G   CARBOHYDRATE 26.4G
CHOLESTEROL 12MG   SODIUM 167MG

Frozen Assets

Make a batch of Refrigerator Yeast Rolls dough to keep in the freezer; you'll have bread whenever you need it. Just follow these steps.
 • Shape the dough into balls as directed.
 • Freeze the balls on a baking sheet. Then put the frozen balls in a heavy-duty, zip-top plastic bag; freeze up to 1 month.
 • To bake, put 12 frozen balls in a cakepan coated with cooking spray; cover and thaw at room temperature 45 minutes or in the refrigerator 8 hours. Let rise; bake as directed.

CHEESE ROLLS

These cheese-filled rolls are best served warm—when the cheese is gooey.

1 package active dry yeast
¼ cup sugar
1¼ cups warm skim milk (105° to 115°)
6¼ cups bread flour, divided
1 cup plain nonfat yogurt
1¼ teaspoons salt
Vegetable cooking spray
4 (¾-ounce) slices American nonfat process
    cheese, each cut into 8 strips
4 (¾-ounce) slices Swiss-flavored nonfat
    process cheese, each cut into 8 strips
1 (5-ounce) package part-skim mozzarella
    string cheese, cut into 32 pieces
1 egg white, lightly beaten
1 teaspoon water
2 tablespoons sesame seeds

Combine first 3 ingredients in a large bowl; let stand 5 minutes. Add 1½ cups flour, yogurt, and salt; stir well. Stir in 3¾ cups flour to make a soft dough. Turn dough out onto a lightly floured surface. Knead until smooth and elastic (10 to 15 minutes); add enough of remaining 1 cup flour, 1 tablespoon at a time, to prevent dough from sticking to hands.

Place dough in a large bowl coated with cooking spray, turning to coat top. Cover and let rise in a warm place (85°), free from drafts, 1 hour or until doubled in bulk. Punch dough down, and divide into 4 equal portions. Working with 1 portion at a time (cover remaining portions to keep from drying out), roll each portion into a 10-inch circle on a lightly floured surface; cut each circle into 8 wedges.

Place 1 strip American cheese, 1 strip Swiss cheese, and 1 piece mozzarella at wide end of each wedge. Fold in corners of wide end about ½ inch; beginning with cheese-filled end, roll up each wedge. Place rolls, point sides down, 2 inches apart on baking sheets coated with cooking spray. Let rise, uncovered, in a warm place (85°), free from drafts, 30 minutes or until doubled in bulk.

Combine egg white and water; stir well. Brush over rolls, and sprinkle with sesame seeds. Bake at 350° for 18 minutes or until golden. Serve warm. Yield: 32 rolls.

PER ROLL: 119 CALORIES (10% FROM FAT)
FAT 1.3G (SATURATED FAT 0.5G)
PROTEIN 5.7G   CARBOHYDRATE 20.6G
CHOLESTEROL 3MG   SODIUM 202MG

Cheese Rolls

Basil-Cheese Rolls

BASIL-CHEESE ROLLS

1 cup warm water (105° to 115°)
1 package active dry yeast
2½ cups bread flour
½ teaspoon salt
1 tablespoon bread flour, divided
Vegetable cooking spray
1 cup loosely packed fresh basil
½ cup chopped onion
3 tablespoons grated Parmesan cheese
1 tablespoon olive oil
¼ teaspoon salt
4 cloves garlic
1 egg white

Combine warm water and yeast in a 1-cup liquid measuring cup; let stand 5 minutes. Position dough blade in food processor bowl; add yeast mixture, 2½ cups bread flour, and ½ teaspoon salt. Process 1 minute or until well blended, stopping once to scrape down sides.

Sprinkle 1½ teaspoons flour evenly over work surface. Turn dough out onto floured surface, and knead until smooth and elastic (about 10 minutes). Place dough in a large bowl coated with cooking spray, turning to coat top. Cover and let rise in a warm place (85°), free from drafts, 45 minutes or until doubled in bulk.

Punch dough down. Sprinkle remaining 1½ teaspoons flour evenly over work surface. Turn dough out onto floured surface, and roll into an 11- x 14-inch rectangle.

Position knife blade in food processor bowl; add basil and remaining 6 ingredients to processor bowl. Process 1 minute or until finely chopped, scraping sides of processor bowl twice. Spread basil pesto mixture evenly over dough. Roll up, starting at long side. Pinch seam to seal (do not seal ends). Cut into 18 (¾-inch) slices. Place slices on a baking sheet coated with cooking spray.

Cover and let rise in a warm place, free from drafts, 20 minutes. Bake at 400° for 15 to 18 minutes or until golden. Yield: 1½ dozen.

PER ROLL: 86 CALORIES (15% FROM FAT)
FAT 1.4G (SATURATED FAT 0.3G)
PROTEIN 3.1G CARBOHYDRATE 15.0G
CHOLESTEROL 1MG SODIUM 114MG

GREEN CHILE PAN ROLLS

2 (4.5-ounce) cans chopped green chiles,
   undrained and divided
¼ cup warm water (105° to 115°)
1 package rapid-rise yeast
1 tablespoon sugar
½ teaspoon salt
⅛ teaspoon ground red pepper
4 cups plus 1 tablespoon all-purpose flour,
   divided
¼ cup stick margarine, divided
⅓ cup cold skim milk
Butter-flavored vegetable cooking spray

Drain 1 can chiles, and press firmly between paper towels to remove excess moisture; set aside.

Combine warm water, yeast, and sugar in a 1-cup liquid measuring cup; let stand 5 minutes.

Position knife blade in food processor bowl. Add remaining 1 can chopped chiles, salt, and pepper; process until smooth. Add 4 cups flour and 3 tablespoons margarine; process 15 seconds.

Add milk to yeast mixture; stir well. Pour yeast mixture through food chute with processor running. Process mixture 30 seconds or until dough forms a ball; process 1 additional minute. Add drained chiles; process 5 seconds. Add remaining 1 tablespoon flour through food chute with processor running; process 5 seconds.

Place dough in a large bowl coated with cooking spray, turning to coat top. Cover and let rise in a warm place (85°), free from drafts, 8 minutes. (Dough will rise slightly.)

Turn dough out onto work surface; divide into 24 equal portions. Shape each portion into a ball. Place balls in two 8-inch round cakepans coated with cooking spray. Cover and let rise in a warm place, free from drafts, 8 minutes. (Rolls will rise slightly.)

Melt remaining 1 tablespoon margarine; brush half of melted margarine over rolls. Bake at 375° for 20 minutes or until golden. Remove rolls from pans, and brush with remaining melted margarine. Yield: 2 dozen.

PER ROLL: 101 CALORIES (20% FROM FAT)
FAT 2.2G (SATURATED FAT 0.4G)
PROTEIN 2.5G CARBOHYDRATE 17.6G
CHOLESTEROL 0MG SODIUM 109MG

DILLWEED ROLLS

*These no-fuss rolls require no kneading.
Simply let the dough rise, spoon it into muffin
pans, let it rise again, and bake.*

1½ cups skim milk
⅓ cup stick margarine
3¾ cups all-purpose flour, divided
¼ cup sugar
2 tablespoons chopped fresh dillweed
½ teaspoon salt
1 package active dry yeast
¼ cup fat-free egg substitute
Vegetable cooking spray

Combine milk and margarine in a saucepan; heat until margarine melts, stirring occasionally. Cool to 120° to 130°.

Combine 1½ cups flour and next 4 ingredients in a large bowl. Gradually add milk mixture to flour mixture, beating well at low speed of an electric mixer. Beat 2 additional minutes at medium speed. Add egg substitute, and beat well. Gradually stir in enough of remaining 2¼ cups flour to make a soft dough (dough will be sticky).

Cover and let rise in a warm place (85°), free from drafts, 45 minutes or until doubled in bulk. Stir dough down to remove air bubbles. Spoon dough into muffin pans coated with cooking spray, filling two-thirds full. Cover and let rise in a warm place, free from drafts, 30 minutes or until doubled in bulk.

Bake at 400° for 15 minutes or until golden. Remove from pans immediately. Serve warm. Yield: 1½ dozen.

PER ROLL: 146 CALORIES (23% FROM FAT)
FAT 3.7G (SATURATED FAT 0.7G)
PROTEIN 3.9G CARBOHYDRATE 23.9G
CHOLESTEROL 0MG SODIUM 121MG

GRAHAM HONEY ROLLS

*Keep variety in the bread basket by shaping the
dough differently each time you prepare these rolls.
Just follow the directions on the facing page.*

3 cups bread flour, divided
¼ cup instant nonfat dry milk powder
¼ teaspoon salt
1 package active dry yeast
1½ cups water
2 tablespoons honey
1 tablespoon stick margarine
1 cup graham flour
1½ tablespoons bread flour
Butter-flavored vegetable cooking spray

Combine 1 cup bread flour and next 3 ingredients in a large mixing bowl, stirring well.

Combine water, honey, and margarine in a saucepan; cook over medium heat until margarine melts, stirring occasionally. Cool to 120° to 130°.

Gradually add honey mixture to flour mixture, beating well at low speed of an electric mixer. Beat 2 additional minutes at medium speed. Gradually stir in graham flour and enough of remaining 2 cups bread flour to make a soft dough.

Sprinkle 1½ tablespoons bread flour evenly over work surface. Turn dough out onto floured surface, and knead until smooth and elastic (about 10 minutes). Place dough in a large bowl coated with cooking spray, turning to coat top. Cover and let rise in a warm place (85°), free from drafts, 45 minutes or until doubled in bulk.

Punch dough down, and divide into 32 equal portions. Roll each portion into a 9-inch rope. Tie each rope in a loose knot, leaving 2 long ends. Place on large baking sheets coated with cooking spray. Cover and let rise in a warm place, free from drafts, 30 minutes or until doubled in bulk.

Bake at 375° for 13 minutes or until golden. Coat rolls lightly with cooking spray. Yield: 32 rolls.

PER ROLL: 74 CALORIES (9% FROM FAT)
FAT 0.7G (SATURATED FAT 0.1G)
PROTEIN 2.6G CARBOHYDRATE 12.1G
CHOLESTEROL 0MG SODIUM 28MG

CLOVERLEAF ROLLS

Coat muffin pans with cooking spray. After first rising, punch dough down, and divide into 4 equal portions. Shape each portion into 21 balls. Place 3 balls in each muffin cup. Cover and let rise until doubled in bulk. Bake as directed. Coat rolls lightly with cooking spray. Yield: 28 rolls.

PER ROLL: 85 CALORIES (8% FROM FAT)
FAT 0.8G (SATURATED FAT 0.1G)
PROTEIN 3.0G CARBOHYDRATE 13.8G
CHOLESTEROL 0MG SODIUM 32MG

Cloverleaf Rolls

CRESCENT ROLLS

After first rising, punch dough down, and divide in half. Place 1 portion on work surface; roll into a 12-inch circle. Cut into 12 wedges; roll each wedge tightly, beginning at wide end. Place rolls, point side down, on a baking sheet coated with cooking spray. Curve into crescent shapes. Repeat procedure with remaining dough. Cover and let rise until doubled in bulk. Bake as directed. Coat rolls lightly with cooking spray. Yield: 2 dozen.

PER ROLL: 99 CALORIES (9% FROM FAT)
FAT 1.0G (SATURATED FAT 0.1G)
PROTEIN 3.5G CARBOHYDRATE 16.1G
CHOLESTEROL 0MG SODIUM 37MG

Crescent Rolls

SPIRAL ROLLS

After first rising, punch dough down, and divide into 32 portions. Roll each portion into a 9-inch rope. Place on baking sheets coated with cooking spray; curl ends in opposite directions. Cover and let rise until doubled in bulk. Bake as directed. Coat rolls lightly with cooking spray. Yield: 32 rolls.

PER ROLL: 74 CALORIES (9% FROM FAT)
FAT 0.7G (SATURATED FAT 0.1G)
PROTEIN 2.6G CARBOHYDRATE 12.1G
CHOLESTEROL 0MG SODIUM 28MG

Spiral Rolls

Cinnamon Rolls

CINNAMON ROLLS

1 cup skim milk
3 tablespoons sugar
1 tablespoon stick margarine
¼ cup warm water (105° to 115°)
1 package active dry yeast
1 egg, lightly beaten
½ teaspoon salt
3¾ cups plus 2 tablespoons bread flour, divided
Vegetable cooking spray
2 tablespoons stick margarine, melted
¼ cup plus 2 tablespoons firmly packed brown
  sugar
2 teaspoons ground cinnamon
1 cup sifted powdered sugar
2 tablespoons skim milk
1 teaspoon vanilla extract

Heat 1 cup milk over medium-high heat in a heavy saucepan to 180° or until tiny bubbles form around edge of pan. (Do not boil.) Remove from heat; add 3 tablespoons sugar and 1 tablespoon margarine, stirring until margarine melts. Cool to 105° to 115°.

Combine warm water and yeast in a 1-cup liquid measuring cup; let stand 5 minutes. Combine milk mixture, yeast mixture, egg, and salt in a large bowl; stir well. Gradually stir in 3½ cups flour to make a soft dough.

Sprinkle 1 tablespoon of remaining flour evenly over work surface. Turn dough out onto floured surface, and knead until smooth and elastic (about 8 minutes). Add enough of remaining ¼ cup plus 1 tablespoon flour, 1 tablespoon at a time, to keep dough from sticking to surface.

Place dough in a bowl coated with cooking spray, turning to coat top. Cover and let rise in a warm place (85°), free from drafts, 1 hour or until doubled in bulk.

Punch dough down. Turn out onto a lightly floured surface; roll to a 20- x 8-inch rectangle. Brush with 2 tablespoons melted margarine. Combine brown sugar and cinnamon; sprinkle over dough. Roll up, starting at long side. Pinch seam to seal (do not seal ends). Cut into 20 (1-inch) slices.

Place slices, cut sides down, in a 13- x 9- x 2-inch pan coated with cooking spray. Cover and let rise in a warm place, free from drafts, 30 minutes or until doubled in bulk.

Bake at 350° for 22 minutes or until done. Combine powdered sugar, 2 tablespoons milk, and vanilla; stir well. Drizzle glaze over hot rolls. Yield: 20 rolls.

PER ROLL: 168 CALORIES (13% FROM FAT)
FAT 2.5G (SATURATED FAT 0.5G)
PROTEIN 4.1G CARBOHYDRATE 32.2G
CHOLESTEROL 11MG SODIUM 91MG

LEMON-GLAZED CRANBERRY ROLLS

Use dental floss or string to cut through the roll of dough. Turn to page 18 to see how.

1 (10-ounce) can refrigerated pizza crust
  dough
½ cup orange marmalade
⅔ cup dried cranberries
Vegetable cooking spray
½ cup sifted powdered sugar
1½ teaspoons lemon juice
1 teaspoon hot water

Unroll pizza dough, and pat into a 12- x 9-inch rectangle. Spread marmalade over dough, leaving a ½-inch border. Sprinkle cranberries over marmalade, pressing gently into dough. Beginning with a long side, roll up, jellyroll fashion; pinch seam to seal (do not seal ends).

Cut roll into 12 (1-inch) slices. Place slices, cut sides up, in muffin pans coated with cooking spray. Bake at 375° for 15 minutes or until golden. Remove rolls from pan, and place on a wire rack.

Combine powdered sugar, lemon juice, and hot water in a small bowl, stirring until smooth. Drizzle glaze over warm rolls. Yield: 1 dozen.

Note: Substitute ⅓ cup apple jelly for orange marmalade and ⅔ cup raisins for cranberries, if desired.

PER ROLL: 155 CALORIES (6% FROM FAT)
FAT 1.0G (SATURATED FAT 0.3G)
PROTEIN 2.9G CARBOHYDRATE 34.7G
CHOLESTEROL 0MG SODIUM 229MG

BAGELS STEP-BY-STEP

1. Punch dough down; divide into 16 equal portions. Shape each portion into a ball; pat each ball into a 3½-inch disk.

2. Poke a hole through the center of each disk of dough.

3. Gently lift each disk, and twirl on your index finger until the hole is 1½ inches in diameter.

4. Place bagels on baking sheets coated with cooking spray. Cover and let rise in a warm place until puffy.

5. Place bagels, one at a time, in simmering water. Immediately turn bagel over; carefully remove from water with a slotted spatula.

6. Place bagels on baking sheets coated with cooking spray; gently brush with egg white mixture, and bake.

BASIC BAGELS

Let the dough for bagels rise until almost doubled in bulk (not completely doubled in bulk). This will keep the bagels dense and chewy.

2 tablespoons sugar
1 package active dry yeast
1½ cups warm water (105° to 115°)
4½ to 5 cups all-purpose flour, divided
1 teaspoon salt
Vegetable cooking spray
1 egg white, lightly beaten
1 teaspoon skim milk

Combine first 3 ingredients in a large bowl; let stand 5 minutes. Stir in 4 cups flour and salt to make a soft dough. Turn dough out onto a lightly floured surface. Knead until smooth and elastic (about 10 minutes); add enough of remaining flour, 1 tablespoon at a time, to prevent dough from sticking to hands. Place dough in a large bowl coated with cooking spray, turning to coat top. Cover and let rise in a warm place (85°), free from drafts, 20 minutes or until almost doubled in bulk.

Punch dough down. Cover and let rest 5 minutes; divide into 16 equal portions; shape each portion into a ball. Pat each ball into a 3½-inch disk. Poke a hole through center of each disk. Gently lift each disk from work surface, and twirl on index finger until hole is 1½ inches in diameter. Place on baking sheets coated with cooking spray. Cover and let rise in a warm place, free from drafts, 20 minutes or until puffy. (Dough will not double in bulk.)

Fill Dutch oven half-full with water. Bring to a boil; reduce heat, and simmer. Add 1 bagel to water. Immediately turn bagel over, and carefully remove from water with a large slotted spatula. Place bagel on a sheet of wax paper coated with cooking spray to drain. Repeat procedure with remaining bagels.

Place bagels on baking sheets coated with cooking spray. Combine egg white and milk; brush over bagels. Bake at 375° for 22 minutes or until golden. Yield: 16 bagels.

PER BAGEL: 138 CALORIES (3% FROM FAT)
FAT 0.5G (SATURATED FAT 0.1G)
PROTEIN 4.0G CARBOHYDRATE 28.6G
CHOLESTEROL 0MG SODIUM 151MG

MINIATURE BASIC BAGELS

Prepare Basic Bagels dough. After first rising, punch dough down; cover and let rest 5 minutes. Divide dough into 32 equal portions; shape each portion into a ball. Working with 1 portion at a time, pat each ball into a 2½-inch disk. Proceed with directions for Basic Bagels. Yield: 32 bagels.

PER BAGEL: 69 CALORIES (4% FROM FAT)
FAT 0.3G (SATURATED FAT 0.0G)
PROTEIN 2.0G CARBOHYDRATE 14.3G
CHOLESTEROL 0MG SODIUM 75MG

POPPY SEED BAGELS

Add 2 teaspoons poppy seeds in with 4 cups flour. Proceed with directions for Basic Bagels. After brushing bagels with egg white mixture, sprinkle 1 teaspoon poppy seeds evenly over bagels. Press seeds gently to adhere. Yield: 16 bagels.

PER BAGEL: 141 CALORIES (5% FROM FAT)
FAT 0.8G (SATURATED FAT 0.1G)
PROTEIN 4.1G CARBOHYDRATE 28.7G
CHOLESTEROL 0MG SODIUM 151MG

CINNAMON-RAISIN BAGELS

Combine ¾ cup raisins and ½ cup water in a saucepan; bring to a boil. Cover, reduce heat, and simmer 1 minute. Remove from heat, and let stand, covered, 30 minutes. Drain and set aside.

Proceed with directions for Basic Bagels, increasing sugar to 3 tablespoons and adding 1 teaspoon ground cinnamon to flour. After turning dough out onto a lightly floured surface, knead raisins into dough. Proceed with directions for Basic Bagels, dividing dough into 19 portions. Yield: 19 bagels.

PER BAGEL: 136 CALORIES (3% FROM FAT)
FAT 0.5G (SATURATED FAT 0.1G)
PROTEIN 3.6G CARBOHYDRATE 29.4G
CHOLESTEROL 0MG SODIUM 128MG

Cheese Breadsticks

CHEESE BREADSTICKS

Freshly grated cheese makes all the difference in this recipe. If you can't find
Romano, use freshly grated Parmesan.

3¼ cups bread flour
¾ cup freshly grated Romano cheese, divided
¼ cup instant nonfat dry milk powder
1 teaspoon salt
1 teaspoon sugar
¼ teaspoon ground red pepper
1 package rapid-rise yeast
1 cup plus 2 tablespoons very warm water
    (120° to 130°)
2 teaspoons olive oil
Vegetable cooking spray
1 egg white, lightly beaten
2 teaspoons water
2 tablespoons cornmeal, divided

Position knife blade in food processor bowl. Add flour, ½ cup cheese, and next 5 ingredients; pulse 6 times or until blended. With processor running, slowly pour very warm water and oil through food chute; process until dough leaves sides of bowl and forms a ball.

Turn dough out onto a floured surface; knead 5 times. Place dough in a large bowl coated with cooking spray, turning to coat top. Cover and let rise in a warm place (85°), free from drafts, 40 minutes or until doubled in bulk.

Combine egg white and 2 teaspoons water; set aside. Coat two baking sheets with cooking spray; sprinkle each with 1 tablespoon cornmeal; set aside.

Punch dough down; turn out onto a floured surface. Divide dough in half; roll 1 portion of dough into a 14- x 10-inch rectangle. Brush half of egg white mixture evenly over rectangle; sprinkle with 2 tablespoons cheese. Using fingertips, press cheese into dough.

Cut rectangle of dough into 22 (10-inch-long) strips. Gently pick up both ends of each strip, and twist dough. Place twisted strips of dough 1 inch apart on a prepared baking sheet. (Dough strips may stretch as they are transferred, creating a unique free-form look.) Repeat procedure with remaining dough, egg white mixture, and cheese.

Cover and let rise in a warm place, free from drafts, 20 minutes or until puffy. Bake at 375° for 12 minutes or until golden. Remove from baking sheets; cool on wire racks. Yield: 44 breadsticks.

PER BREADSTICK: 51 CALORIES (16% FROM FAT)
FAT 0.9G (SATURATED FAT 0.4G)
PROTEIN 2.2G CARBOHYDRATE 8.2G
CHOLESTEROL 2MG SODIUM 82MG

Carefully pick up both ends of each strip; twist dough. Lay strips on a baking sheet.

GARLIC-MUSTARD SOFT PRETZELS

1½ cups all-purpose flour, divided
1 cup whole wheat flour
1 package active dry yeast
1 tablespoon sugar
½ teaspoon salt
½ teaspoon garlic powder
½ teaspoon dry mustard
1 cup water
1 tablespoon stick margarine
2 tablespoons all-purpose flour
Vegetable cooking spray
1 egg white, lightly beaten
2 teaspoons water
2 teaspoons wheat germ

Combine ½ cup all-purpose flour and next 6 ingredients in a large bowl; stir well. Set aside.

Combine 1 cup water and margarine in a saucepan; cook over medium heat until very warm (120° to 130°). Add to yeast mixture, beating at low speed of an electric mixer until blended. Beat 3 minutes at medium speed. Stir in enough of remaining 1 cup all-purpose flour to make a soft dough.

Sprinkle 2 tablespoons all-purpose flour over work surface. Turn dough out onto floured surface; knead until smooth and elastic (8 to 10 minutes). Place dough in a bowl coated with cooking spray; turn to coat top. Cover; let rise in a warm place (85°), free from drafts, 45 minutes or until doubled in bulk.

Punch dough down; cover and let rest 15 minutes. Divide dough in half. Working with 1 portion at a time, divide each portion into 8 pieces; roll each piece into a 14-inch rope. Twist each rope into a pretzel shape. Place pretzels on baking sheets coated with cooking spray.

Cover and let rise in a warm place, free from drafts, 20 minutes or until doubled in bulk. Combine egg white and 2 teaspoons water; brush over pretzels. Sprinkle with wheat germ. Bake at 400° for 10 minutes or until golden. Yield: 16 pretzels.

PER PRETZEL: 83 CALORIES (12% FROM FAT)
FAT 1.1G (SATURATED FAT 0.8G)
PROTEIN 2.8G CARBOHYDRATE 15.6G
CHOLESTEROL 0MG SODIUM 86MG

Parmesan Ribbon Bread (recipe on page 67)

SENSATIONAL YEAST LOAVES

*I*f you've shied away from making yeast breads because you thought they were too difficult, this chapter is for you. The recipes and instructional photos will help you easily master the techniques of working with yeast.

Just turn to page 58 to find one of the most versatile breads, Tender Yeast Bread. You can serve it as a basic bread or use its dough to make one of three spectacular variations. Recipes for white, whole wheat, and rye breads fill the pages—and flavorings such as cinnamon, cheese, pepper, and herbs sweeten and spice up the breads.

On days when you simply have too little time to wait for the bread to rise, you can still have homemade yeast bread, thanks to the convenience of commercial bread products. Honey-flavored Almond French Bread (page 62) and Sweet Onion and Poppy Seed Focaccia (page 69) call for refrigerated French bread dough. Homemade yeast bread has never been so easy.

TENDER YEAST BREAD

You can use this dough to make the two breads that follow as well as a delicious coffee cake, Raspberry-Pecan Tea Ring (page 73).

1½ cups warm water (105° to 115°)
2 packages active dry yeast
1 tablespoon sugar
6 cups bread flour, divided
½ cup instant nonfat dry milk powder
¼ cup vegetable oil
¼ cup honey
1½ teaspoons salt
1 egg
Vegetable cooking spray

Combine first 3 ingredients in a 2-cup liquid measuring cup; let stand 5 minutes. Combine yeast mixture, 2 cups flour, and next 5 ingredients in a large mixing bowl; beat at medium speed of an electric mixer until well blended. Gradually stir in 3 cups flour to make a soft dough.

Sprinkle ½ cup of remaining flour over work surface. Turn dough out onto floured surface; knead until smooth and elastic (about 10 minutes). Add enough of remaining ½ cup flour, 1 tablespoon at a time, to keep dough from sticking to hands.

Place dough in a large bowl coated with cooking spray, turning to coat top. Cover and let rise in a warm place (85°), free from drafts, 1 hour or until doubled in bulk.

Punch dough down; turn out onto a floured surface. Cover; let rest 10 minutes. Divide dough in half; roll 1 portion into a 14- x 8-inch rectangle. Roll up, starting at short side, pressing to eliminate air pockets; pinch ends to seal. Place dough, seam side down, in a 9- x 5- x 3-inch loafpan coated with cooking spray. Repeat with remaining dough.

Cover and let rise in a warm place, free from drafts, 40 minutes or until doubled in bulk. Bake at 350° for 30 minutes or until loaves sound hollow when tapped. Remove from pans, and cool on wire racks. Yield: 2 loaves, 18 (½-inch) slices each.

PER SLICE: 114 CALORIES (17% FROM FAT)
FAT 2.1G (SATURATED FAT 0.4G)
PROTEIN 3.7G CARBOHYDRATE 19.9G
CHOLESTEROL 6MG SODIUM 110MG

To braid dough for Peppercorn-Cheese Braids, pinch the ends of three ropes of dough together, and braid. At the end of the braid, pinch the ends together, and tuck them under for a smooth, round end.

PEPPERCORN-CHEESE BRAIDS

This top-rated, savory variation of Tender Yeast Bread is perfect as part of any holiday dinner.

Tender Yeast Bread dough (at left)
1 tablespoon plus 2 teaspoons coarsely ground pepper, divided
¾ cup grated Romano cheese
⅔ cup no-salt-added whole-kernel corn, drained
2 tablespoons bread flour
Vegetable cooking spray
1 egg white, lightly beaten
2 teaspoons water

Prepare dough for Tender Yeast Bread, adding 1 tablespoon plus 1½ teaspoons pepper, cheese, and corn to dough mixture with dry milk powder. Sprinkle 2 tablespoons flour over work surface. After first rising, punch dough down, and turn out onto floured surface; cover and let rest 10 minutes.

Divide dough into 6 equal portions; shape each portion into a 20-inch rope. Place 3 ropes side by side on a baking sheet coated with cooking spray (do not stretch); pinch ropes together at 1 end to seal. Braid ropes; pinch loose ends to seal. Repeat procedure with remaining 3 ropes of dough. Let rise, uncovered, in a warm place (85°), free from drafts, 40 minutes or until doubled in bulk.

Combine egg white and water; brush over braids. Sprinkle with remaining ½ teaspoon pepper. Bake at 350° for 20 to 25 minutes or until braids sound hollow when tapped. Cool on a wire rack. Yield: 2 loaves, 17 (1-inch) slices each.

PER SLICE: 146 CALORIES (22% FROM FAT)
FAT 3.6G (SATURATED FAT 1.3G)
PROTEIN 5.8G CARBOHYDRATE 22.4G
CHOLESTEROL 12MG SODIUM 178MG

CINNAMON SWIRL BREAD

(pictured on cover)

Like Peppercorn-Cheese Braids, this bread got a perfect score from the test kitchens. Unlike the braids, though, it is sweet—and ideal for breakfast or brunch.

Tender Yeast Bread dough (facing page)
2 tablespoons bread flour
1 egg white, lightly beaten
2 teaspoons water
¼ cup sugar
1 tablespoon plus 1 teaspoon ground
    cinnamon
⅛ teaspoon ground cloves
Vegetable cooking spray
¾ cup sifted powdered sugar
1 tablespoon skim milk
½ teaspoon vanilla extract

Prepare dough for Tender Yeast Bread. Sprinkle 2 tablespoons flour over work surface. After first rising, punch dough down, and turn out onto floured surface; cover and let rest 10 minutes.

Combine egg white and water; set aside. Combine ¼ cup sugar, cinnamon, and cloves; set aside.

Divide dough in half; roll 1 portion into a 14- x 8-inch rectangle. Brush half of egg white mixture over rectangle; sprinkle with half of cinnamon mixture. Roll up dough, starting at short side,

pressing firmly to eliminate air pockets; pinch ends to seal.

Place dough, seam side down, in a 9- x 5-x 3-inch loafpan coated with cooking spray. Repeat procedure with remaining dough, egg white mixture, and cinnamon mixture.

Cover and let rise in a warm place (85°), free from drafts, 40 minutes or until doubled in bulk. Bake at 350° for 30 minutes or until loaves sound hollow when tapped. Remove bread from pans immediately; cool on wire racks.

Combine powdered sugar, milk, and vanilla in a small bowl; stir well. Drizzle over loaves. Yield: 2 loaves, 18 (½-inch) slices each.

PER SLICE: 130 CALORIES (15% FROM FAT)
FAT 2.1G (SATURATED FAT 0.4G)
PROTEIN 3.8G CARBOHYDRATE 23.9G
CHOLESTEROL 7MG SODIUM 111MG

Start at the short side of the rectangle, and roll up dough. Press dough firmly as you roll to push out air pockets; then pinch dough at both ends to seal in the filling.

Cracked Wheat and Honey Loaf

CRACKED WHEAT AND HONEY LOAVES

2 cups boiling water
⅔ cup bulgur (cracked wheat), uncooked
⅔ cup warm water (105° to 115°)
2 envelopes active dry yeast
4½ cups all-purpose flour, divided
3 cups whole wheat flour, divided
¾ cup honey
1 tablespoon salt
3 tablespoons corn oil
Vegetable cooking spray
1 tablespoon stick margarine, melted

Pour boiling water over bulgur in a large bowl. Set aside; cool to 105° to 115°.

Combine warm water and yeast in a 1-cup liquid measuring cup; let stand 5 minutes.

Add yeast mixture, 2 cups all-purpose flour, 2 cups whole wheat flour, and next 3 ingredients to bulgur mixture. Beat at low speed of an electric mixer 1 minute or until blended; beat at medium speed 3 minutes. Gradually stir in remaining 1 cup whole wheat flour and enough of remaining 2½ cups all-purpose flour to make a soft dough.

Turn dough out onto a lightly floured surface. Knead until dough is smooth and elastic (about 10 minutes), adding only enough all-purpose flour to keep dough from sticking to hands.

Place dough in large bowl coated with cooking spray, turning to coat top. Cover and let rise in a warm place (85°), free from drafts, 1 hour or until doubled in bulk.

Punch dough down. Divide dough in half. Roll 1 portion to a 12- x 8-inch rectangle on a lightly floured surface. Roll up dough, starting with short end. Press seam together; pinch ends, and tuck under loaf. Repeat procedure with remaining dough. Coat two 9- x 5- x 3-inch loafpans with cooking spray; place loaves in pans. Cover and let rise in warm place, free from drafts, 45 minutes or until doubled in bulk.

Bake at 350° for 40 minutes or until loaves are browned and sound hollow when tapped. Cover loosely with aluminum foil during last 10 minutes, if necessary, to prevent excessive browning. Remove loaves from pans. Brush with margarine; cool on wire racks. Yield: 2 loaves, 18 (½-inch) slices each.

PER SLICE: 138 CALORIES (12% FROM FAT)
FAT 1.9G (SATURATED FAT 0.3G)
PROTEIN 3.5G   CARBOHYDRATE 27.4G
CHOLESTEROL 0MG   SODIUM 200MG

HARVEST BREAD

(pictured on page 2)

2 packages active dry yeast
1⅔ cups warm skim milk (105° to 115°)
3⅓ cups bread flour, divided
1½ cups rye flour
1½ cups whole wheat flour
1 cup stone-ground cornmeal
¾ cup cooked, mashed or canned pumpkin
⅓ cup molasses
2 tablespoons stick margarine, melted
1½ teaspoons salt
Vegetable cooking spray

Combine yeast and warm milk in a large bowl; let stand 5 minutes. Add 2⅔ cups bread flour and next 7 ingredients, stirring until a soft dough forms.

Turn dough out onto a well-floured surface; knead until smooth and elastic (about 15 minutes). Add enough of remaining ⅔ cup bread flour to keep dough from sticking to hands. Place in a large bowl coated with cooking spray, turning to coat top. Cover and let rise in a warm place (85°), free from drafts, 1 hour or until doubled in bulk.

Punch dough down, and divide in half; roll 1 portion into a 15- x 7-inch rectangle. Roll up, starting at short side, pressing to eliminate air pockets; pinch ends to seal. Place loaf, seam side down, in an 8½- x 4½- x 3-inch loafpan coated with cooking spray. Repeat procedure with remaining dough.

Cover and let rise in a warm place, free from drafts, 40 minutes or until doubled in bulk. Bake at 375° for 35 minutes or until loaves sound hollow when tapped. Remove bread from pans; cool on wire racks. Yield: 2 loaves, 16 (½-inch) slices each.

PER SLICE: 127 CALORIES (9% FROM FAT)
FAT 1.3G (SATURATED FAT 0.2G)
PROTEIN 3.9G   CARBOHYDRATE 25.0G
CHOLESTEROL 0MG   SODIUM 127MG

FRENCH WHEAT BAGUETTES

1½ cups warm water (105° to 115°), divided
1 package active dry yeast
1 teaspoon sugar
3¼ cups bread flour
1 cup whole wheat flour
1½ teaspoons salt
Vegetable cooking spray
1 tablespoon cornmeal

Combine ½ cup warm water, yeast, and sugar in a 1-cup liquid measuring cup; let stand 5 minutes.

Position knife blade in food processor bowl; add bread flour, whole wheat flour, and salt. Pulse 4 times or until blended. With processor running, slowly add yeast mixture and remaining 1 cup warm water through food chute; process until dough leaves sides of bowl and forms a ball. Process 15 additional seconds.

Turn dough out onto a lightly floured surface; knead 3 or 4 times. Place dough in a large bowl coated with cooking spray, turning to coat top. Cover and let rise in a warm place (85°), free from drafts, 45 minutes or until doubled in bulk.

Punch dough down, and turn out onto a lightly floured surface; knead 3 or 4 times. Cover and let rest 5 minutes. Divide dough in half; roll each portion into a 17- x 9-inch rectangle. Roll up each rectangle, starting with a long edge, pressing firmly to eliminate air pockets; pinch ends to seal. Place each roll, seam side down, in an 18-inch-long baguette pan coated with cooking spray and sprinkled with cornmeal. Cover and let rise 45 minutes or until doubled in bulk.

Uncover dough; using a sharp knife, make 6 diagonal cuts ¼ inch deep across top of loaves. Spray loaves lightly with water. Bake at 400° for 25 minutes or until loaves sound hollow when tapped. Remove from pans; cool on wire racks. Yield: 2 loaves, 12 slices each.

PER SLICE: 76 CALORIES (5% FROM FAT)
FAT 0.4G (SATURATED FAT 0.0G)
PROTEIN 2.6G CARBOHYDRATE 15.4G
CHOLESTEROL 0MG SODIUM 147MG

ALMOND FRENCH BREAD

You don't need a floured surface when working with commercial refrigerated dough. Braid it on the countertop or directly on the baking sheet.

1 (11-ounce) can refrigerated French bread dough
Vegetable cooking spray
2 tablespoons honey
½ teaspoon water
⅛ teaspoon ground ginger
2 tablespoons sliced almonds

Unroll dough; cut lengthwise into 3 equal pieces. Shape each portion into a rope. Place ropes on a baking sheet coated with cooking spray (do not stretch). Braid ropes; pinch loose ends to seal. Combine honey, water, and ginger, stirring well. Brush dough with half of honey mixture.

Bake at 350° for 20 minutes. Remove from oven; brush with remaining honey mixture, and sprinkle with almonds. Bake 10 additional minutes or until loaf sounds hollow when tapped. Remove bread from baking sheet immediately. Serve warm. Yield: 1 loaf, 10 slices.

PER SLICE: 97 CALORIES (17% FROM FAT)
FAT 1.8G (SATURATED FAT 0.6G)
PROTEIN 3.3G CARBOHYDRATE 17.3G
CHOLESTEROL 0MG SODIUM 195MG

SESAME-GARLIC FRENCH BREAD

Shape dough as directed above. Omit honey, water, ginger, and almonds. Cut 2 cloves garlic into thin slices, and insert slices evenly into braid. Brush 1½ tablespoons melted reduced-calorie stick margarine over braid, and sprinkle with 2 teaspoons sesame seeds. Bake at 350° for 25 minutes or until loaf sounds hollow when tapped. Remove from baking sheet immediately. Serve warm. Yield: 1 loaf, 10 slices.

PER SLICE: 86 CALORIES (23% FROM FAT)
FAT 2.2G (SATURATED FAT 0.7G)
PROTEIN 3.1G CARBOHYDRATE 13.7G
CHOLESTEROL 0MG SODIUM 212MG

Almond French Bread

English Muffin Bread

ENGLISH MUFFIN BREAD

The only unusual equipment needed for baking this bread is three coffee cans.

6 cups all-purpose flour, divided
1 tablespoon sugar
2 teaspoons salt
¼ teaspoon baking soda
2 packages active dry yeast
2 cups 1% low-fat milk
½ cup water
Vegetable cooking spray
1 tablespoon yellow cornmeal, divided

Combine 3 cups flour and next 4 ingredients in a large bowl; stir well, and set aside.

Heat milk and water in a heavy saucepan until very warm (120° to 130°). Add to flour mixture, stirring well. Stir in remaining 3 cups flour to make a soft dough.

Divide dough into 3 equal portions. Place 1 portion in each of three 13-ounce coffee cans coated with cooking spray and each sprinkled with ¾ teaspoon cornmeal. Sprinkle remaining cornmeal over dough. Cover; let rise in a warm place (85°), free from drafts, 45 minutes or until doubled in bulk.

Bake at 400° for 20 minutes. Remove bread from cans; serve. Yield: 3 loaves, 10 (½-inch) slices each.

PER SERVING: 95 CALORIES (4% FROM FAT)
FAT 0.4G (SATURATED FAT 0.1G)
PROTEIN 3.1G   CARBOHYDRATE 19.2G
CHOLESTEROL 1MG   SODIUM 172MG

BEER-CHEESE BREAD

¾ cup beer
¼ cup stick margarine
3½ cups bread flour, divided
1 tablespoon sugar
½ teaspoon salt
½ teaspoon dry mustard
¼ teaspoon ground red pepper
1 package active dry yeast
1 egg
1 cup (4 ounces) shredded reduced-fat sharp
    Cheddar cheese
Vegetable cooking spray

Combine beer and margarine in a small sauce-pan; cook over medium-low heat until very warm (120° to 130°).

Combine 1½ cups flour and next 5 ingredients in a large bowl. Add beer mixture and egg; beat at medium speed of an electric mixer until smooth. Stir in cheese and 1½ cups flour to make a soft dough.

Turn dough out onto a lightly floured surface. Knead until smooth and elastic (about 8 minutes); add enough of remaining ½ cup flour, 1 tablespoon at a time, to keep dough from sticking to hands. Place in a large bowl coated with cooking spray, turning to coat top. Cover dough, and let rise in a warm place (85°), free from drafts, 1 hour or until doubled in bulk.

Punch dough down; cover and let rest 10 minutes. Place in a 1-quart soufflé dish coated with cooking spray. Cover dough, and let rise 40 minutes or until doubled in bulk. Uncover and bake at 375° for 20 minutes. Cover loosely with aluminum foil; bake 20 additional minutes or until loaf sounds hollow when tapped. Remove loaf from dish; cool on a wire rack. Cut into wedges. Yield: 1 loaf, 16 wedges.

PER WEDGE: 150 CALORIES (29% FROM FAT)
FAT 4.8G (SATURATED FAT 1.5G)
PROTEIN 5.3G CARBOHYDRATE 20.9G
CHOLESTEROL 18MG SODIUM 163MG

Beer-Cheese Bread

Italian Spinach-Cheese Twists

3 tablespoons olive oil
1 large clove garlic, minced
2 packages active dry yeast
1 tablespoon sugar
2 cups warm water (105° to 115°)
5¼ cups bread flour, divided
1½ teaspoons salt
Vegetable cooking spray
1 (10-ounce) package frozen chopped spinach,
   thawed and well drained
½ cup freshly grated Parmesan cheese
1 teaspoon dried Italian seasoning
1 egg white, lightly beaten
1 tablespoon water

Combine oil and garlic in a small bowl. Microwave at HIGH 1 minute; cool. Combine yeast, sugar, and warm water; let stand 5 minutes.

Combine 3 cups flour and salt in a large bowl. Add garlic mixture and yeast mixture; stir until well blended. Add 2 cups flour, stirring until a soft dough forms.

Turn dough out into a lightly floured surface. Knead until smooth and elastic (about 8 minutes); add enough of remaining ¼ cup flour, 1 tablespoon at a time, to keep dough from sticking to hands. Place dough in a large bowl coated with cooking spray, turning to coat top. Cover and let rise in a warm place (85°), free from drafts, 45 minutes or until doubled in bulk.

Punch dough down; turn out onto a lightly floured surface, and let rest 5 minutes. Divide dough in half. Roll each portion into a 15- x 10-inch rectangle. Combine spinach, cheese, and Italian seasoning; stir well. Arrange spinach mixture evenly over each rectangle, leaving a ½-inch margin around edges. Roll up each rectangle, starting with a long edge, pressing to eliminate air pockets; pinch ends to seal. Place rolls, seam sides up, on opposite ends of a large baking sheet coated with cooking spray.

Working with 1 roll at a time, fold roll in half, placing 1 half directly on top of other half; pinch ends to seal. Using kitchen shears, cut through folded end of roll, cutting through roll to within 1 inch of opposite end. Twist cut halves of dough outward so that filling faces up. Repeat procedure with remaining roll. Cover and let rise 1 hour or until doubled in bulk.

Combine egg white and 1 tablespoon water; brush over loaves. Bake at 350° for 20 minutes or until loaves sound hollow when tapped. Remove from pan, and cool on wire racks. Yield: 2 loaves, 20 slices each.

Per Slice: 84 Calories (18% from Fat)
Fat 1.7g (Saturated Fat 0.4g)
Protein 3.1g   Carbohydrate 13.9g
Cholesterol 1mg   Sodium 118mg

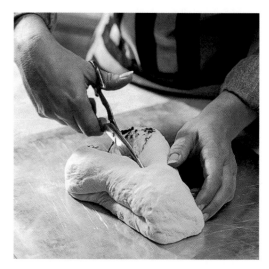

Cut through folded end of roll to within 1 inch of opposite end. Twist cut halves of dough outward so that filling faces up.

PARMESAN RIBBON BREAD

(pictured on page 56)

1¼ cups warm water (105° to 115°), divided
1 package active dry yeast
1 teaspoon sugar
3½ cups bread flour, divided
½ teaspoon salt
1 tablespoon olive oil
2 teaspoons bread flour
Vegetable cooking spray
1 egg white, lightly beaten
1 tablespoon water
½ cup plus 1 tablespoon grated Parmesan
    cheese, divided
1½ teaspoons dried Italian seasoning, divided
1½ teaspoons coarsely ground pepper, divided

Combine ¼ cup warm water, yeast, and sugar in a 1-cup liquid measuring cup; let stand 5 minutes.

Combine 2 cups flour and salt in a large mixing bowl; stir well. Add yeast mixture, remaining 1 cup warm water, and oil; beat at medium speed of an electric mixer until blended. Beat 2 additional minutes at medium speed. Gradually stir in enough of remaining 1½ cups flour to make a soft dough.

Sprinkle 2 teaspoons flour evenly over work surface. Turn dough out onto floured surface; knead until smooth and elastic (8 to 10 minutes). Place dough in a large bowl coated with cooking spray, turning to coat top. Cover and let rise in a warm place (85°), free from drafts, 45 minutes or until doubled in bulk.

Punch down dough; set aside one-fourth of dough. Divide remaining dough into 2 equal portions. Roll each portion to a 12- x 9-inch rectangle. Combine egg white and 1 tablespoon water; brush over rectangles. Sprinkle each rectangle with 3 tablespoons cheese, ½ teaspoon Italian seasoning, and ½ teaspoon pepper. Gently press cheese and herbs into dough, using a rolling pin. Fold each rectangle lengthwise into thirds. Pinch seam and ends to seal.

Roll reserved one-fourth of dough to a 20- x 6-inch rectangle; brush with egg white mixture. Sprinkle with remaining 3 tablespoons cheese,

½ teaspoon Italian seasoning, and ½ teaspoon pepper. Gently press cheese and herbs into dough, using a rolling pin. Cut rectangle into 4 equal lengthwise strips.

With cheese side facing down, attach 1 strip of dough at 1 end of 1 loaf; wrap dough strip clockwise around loaf. Attach second strip where first strip began; wrap strip counter-clockwise to form a crisscross pattern around loaf. Pinch strip at ends to fasten securely. Repeat procedure with remaining loaf and strips.

Cover and let rise in a warm place, free from drafts, 50 minutes or until doubled in bulk. Brush loaves lightly with egg white mixture. Bake at 375° for 25 to 30 minutes or until loaves sound hollow when tapped. Yield: 2 loaves, 12 (1-inch) slices each.

PER SLICE: 90 CALORIES (15% FROM FAT)
FAT 1.5G (SATURATED FAT 0.5G)
PROTEIN 3.5G   CARBOHYDRATE 15.2G
CHOLESTEROL 1MG   SODIUM 87MG

Storing Bread

Contrary to popular belief, bread will become stale more quickly when stored in the refrigerator than at room temperature. If you want to store bread for just two or three days, cool it completely; then cover with airtight wrap, and store at room temperature. (If not eaten within a few days, homemade bread will mold at room temperature.)

For longer storage, wrap the cooled bread tightly in aluminum foil, place in a freezer bag, and freeze up to three months. To serve, partially unwrap bread; let it stand at room temperature until thawed. Place thawed bread on a baking sheet; bake, uncovered, at 350° for 5 to 15 minutes or until heated thoroughly, depending on the size and density of the bread.

RICOTTA CASSEROLE BREAD

This dough requires no kneading and rises only once, which reduces the preparation time. It is slightly coarser than kneaded bread dough.

1 cup part-skim ricotta cheese
2 tablespoons sugar
2 tablespoons instant minced onion
2 tablespoons reduced-calorie stick margarine, melted
1 teaspoon baking powder
¼ teaspoon salt
1 cup warm water (105° to 115°)
2 packages active dry yeast
2 teaspoons sugar
3¼ cups all-purpose flour, divided
½ cup instant potato flakes
Vegetable cooking spray

Combine first 6 ingredients in a large mixing bowl, stirring well.

Combine warm water, yeast, and 2 teaspoons sugar in a 2-cup liquid measuring cup; let stand 5 minutes. Add yeast mixture to ricotta cheese mixture, and stir well.

Add 2 cups flour and potato flakes to yeast mixture; beat at low speed of an electric mixer until well blended. Beat 2 additional minutes at medium speed. Gradually stir in remaining 1¼ cups flour.

Place dough in a large bowl coated with cooking spray, turning to coat top. Cover and let rise in a warm place (85°), free from drafts, 40 to 45 minutes or until doubled in bulk.

Punch dough down, and shape into a ball. Place dough in a 2-quart deep casserole coated with cooking spray. Bake at 350° for 50 minutes or until loaf sounds hollow when tapped. Remove from casserole immediately, and cool on a wire rack. To serve, cut into wedges. Yield: 1 loaf, 18 wedges.

PER WEDGE: 115 CALORIES (13% FROM FAT)
FAT 1.6G (SATURATED FAT 0.4G)
PROTEIN 4.2G CARBOHYDRATE 21.5G
CHOLESTEROL 2MG SODIUM 80MG

PLAIN FOCACCIA

3 cups bread flour
1 teaspoon sugar
1 teaspoon salt
1 package active dry yeast
¾ cup plus 2 tablespoons warm water (105° to 115°)
2 tablespoons plus 1 teaspoon olive oil, divided
Vegetable cooking spray
1 tablespoon cornmeal

Position knife blade in food processor bowl; add first 4 ingredients, and pulse 2 times or until blended. With processor running, slowly add warm water and 2 tablespoons oil through food chute; process until dough leaves sides of bowl and forms a ball. Process 1 additional minute.

Turn dough out onto a lightly floured surface, and knead 4 or 5 times; shape into a ball. Remove metal blade from processor bowl. Poke a hole through the center of ball of dough; return to processor bowl. Coat dough with cooking spray; cover bowl with heavy-duty plastic wrap.

Fill a 1-cup glass measuring cup with water, and place in back of microwave oven. Place processor bowl in center of microwave oven. Microwave at LOW (10% power) 3 minutes; let stand, covered, in microwave 3 minutes. Repeat procedures 2 times, allowing 6 minutes for last standing time.

Turn dough out onto a lightly floured surface; knead 4 or 5 times, and shape into a ball. Coat dough with cooking spray; cover and let rest 10 minutes. Roll dough into a 14-inch circle; place on a baking sheet sprinkled with cornmeal. Brush dough with remaining 1 teaspoon oil. Cover with heavy-duty plastic wrap; let rise in a warm place (85°), free from drafts, 25 minutes or until puffy.

Using handle of a wooden spoon or fingertips, make indentations in top of dough. Bake at 400° for 18 minutes or until browned. Cut focaccia into wedges, and serve warm. Yield: 14 wedges.

PER WEDGE: 136 (19% FROM FAT)
FAT 2.9G (SATURATED FAT 0.4G)
PROTEIN 3.9G CARBOHYDRATE 23.1G
CHOLESTEROL 0MG SODIUM 168MG

POLENTA FOCACCIA
Plain Focaccia (facing page)
¼ cup yellow cornmeal

Prepare dough for Plain Focaccia, adding ¼ cup yellow cornmeal to 3 cups flour. Yield: 14 wedges.

PER WEDGE: 145 CALORIES (18% FROM FAT)
FAT 2.9G (SATURATED FAT 0.4G)
PROTEIN 4.1G CARBOHYDRATE 25.0G
CHOLESTEROL 0MG SODIUM 169MG

SWEET ONION AND POPPY SEED FOCACCIA

Many Italian restaurants serve focaccia with their meals instead of traditional loaves of bread. Here's a supereasy version that's topped with seasoned cooked onions.

1 pound Vidalia or other sweet onions
Vegetable cooking spray
2 tablespoons chopped fresh parsley
1 teaspoon poppy seeds
¼ teaspoon salt
⅛ teaspoon pepper
1 (11-ounce) can refrigerated French bread
   dough

Peel onions, and cut in half lengthwise. Cut each half crosswise into thin slices.

Coat a large nonstick skillet with cooking spray; place over medium-high heat until hot. Add onion; sauté 8 minutes or until golden. Remove from heat; stir in parsley and next 3 ingredients.

Unroll bread dough, and place on a baking sheet coated with cooking spray; pat into a 16- x 7-inch rectangle. Spread onion mixture over dough, leaving a ½-inch border. Bake at 350° for 25 minutes or until golden. Remove from pan; cool 5 minutes on a wire rack. Serve warm. Yield: 8 servings.

PER SERVING: 140 CALORIES (10% FROM FAT)
FAT 1.5G (SATURATED FAT 0.3G)
PROTEIN 5.5G CARBOHYDRATE 26.4G
CHOLESTEROL 0MG SODIUM 344MG

TOMATO, BASIL, AND ANCHOVY FOCACCIA

Polenta Focaccia (at left)
2 large ripe unpeeled tomatoes, thinly sliced
   (about 1 pound)
1 tablespoon minced fresh basil
8 canned anchovy fillets, chopped (about
   ¾ ounce)
½ teaspoon freshly ground pepper

Prepare dough for Polenta Focaccia; roll into a 14-inch circle. Place on a baking sheet sprinkled with cornmeal. After making indentations in dough, top with tomato slices, basil, and anchovies; sprinkle with pepper.

Bake at 400° for 20 minutes or until lightly browned. Cut into wedges, and serve warm. Yield: 14 wedges.

PER WEDGE: 153 (19% FROM FAT)
FAT 3.2G (SATURATED FAT 0.4G)
PROTEIN 4.8G CARBOHYDRATE 26.2G
CHOLESTEROL 0MG SODIUM 228MG

Tomato, Basil, and Anchovy Focaccia

Hawaiian Bubble Bread

HAWAIIAN BUBBLE BREAD

1 cup warm water (105° to 115°)
2 packages active dry yeast
1 teaspoon sugar
1 cup sliced ripe banana
½ cup pineapple-orange-banana juice
   concentrate, thawed and undiluted
¼ cup honey
2 tablespoons stick margarine, melted
2 drops yellow food coloring (optional)
5¼ cups bread flour, divided
1 teaspoon salt
Vegetable cooking spray
¼ cup cream of coconut
2 tablespoons pineapple-orange-banana juice
   concentrate, thawed and undiluted
½ cup sifted powdered sugar

Combine first 3 ingredients in a 2-cup liquid measuring cup; let stand 5 minutes.

Combine banana and next 3 ingredients in container of an electric blender; add food coloring, if desired. Cover and process until smooth, stopping once to scrape down sides.

Combine 2 cups flour and salt in a large bowl; stir well. Add yeast mixture and banana mixture, stirring until well blended. Add 2¾ cups flour, stirring to make a soft dough.

Turn dough out onto a lightly floured surface, and knead until smooth and elastic (about 8 minutes). Add enough of remaining ½ cup flour, 1 tablespoon at a time, to keep dough from sticking to hands.

Place dough in a large bowl coated with cooking spray, turning to coat top. Cover and let rise in a warm place (85°), free from drafts, 1 hour or until doubled in bulk.

Punch dough down; turn out onto a lightly floured surface. Cover and let rest 5 minutes. Shape dough into 1½-inch balls (about 30 balls) on a lightly floured surface. Layer balls in a 10-inch tube pan coated with cooking spray; set aside.

Combine cream of coconut and 2 tablespoons juice concentrate in a bowl; stir well. Pour 3 tablespoons juice mixture over dough, and set aside

remaining juice mixture. Cover dough, and let rise in a warm place, free from drafts, 45 minutes or until doubled in bulk.

Bake at 350° for 30 minutes or until loaf sounds hollow when tapped. Cool in pan 20 minutes. Remove from pan; place on a wire rack. Stir powdered sugar into reserved juice mixture; drizzle over warm bread. Yield: 30 servings.

PER SERVING: 126 CALORIES (14% FROM FAT)
FAT 1.9G (SATURATED FAT 0.8G)
PROTEIN 3.2G   CARBOHYDRATE 24.0G
CHOLESTEROL 0MG   SODIUM 88MG

Layer balls of dough in a 10-inch tube pan coated with cooking spray.

Fresh Cherry Breakfast Bread

FRESH CHERRY BREAKFAST BREAD

2 cups pitted, chopped sweet cherries (about
    ¾ pound)
½ cup water
¼ cup sugar
1 teaspoon almond extract
1 cup skim milk
½ cup mashed cooked potato
2 tablespoons stick margarine
4¾ cups bread flour, divided
¼ cup sugar
½ teaspoon salt
1 package active dry yeast
Vegetable cooking spray
1 egg white, lightly beaten
1 tablespoon sliced almonds
1 tablespoon sugar

Combine first 3 ingredients in a small saucepan;
bring to a boil. Reduce heat; simmer, uncovered, 7

minutes or until thickened, stirring constantly.
Remove from heat; stir in almond extract. Cool.

Heat milk over medium-high heat in a heavy
saucepan to 180° or until tiny bubbles form around
edge. (Do not boil.) Remove from heat; add potato
and margarine, stirring until margarine melts. Cool
until very warm (120° to 130°).

Combine 2 cups flour and next 3 ingredients in a
large bowl; stir well. Add milk mixture; stir until
smooth. Add 2 cups flour, stirring until a stiff
dough forms.

Turn dough out onto a lightly floured surface.
Knead until smooth and elastic (about 8 minutes);
add enough remaining ¾ cup flour, 1 tablespoon at
a time, to keep dough from sticking to hands.
Place dough in a large bowl coated with cooking
spray, turning to coat top. Cover and let rise in a
warm place (85°), free from drafts, 1 hour or until
doubled in bulk.

Punch dough down, and turn out onto a lightly
floured surface. Knead 4 or 5 times. Roll dough
into a 16- x 8-inch rectangle. Place on baking sheet
coated with cooking spray. Spread cherry mixture
lengthwise down center third of dough. Make
diagonal cuts, 1 inch apart, on opposite sides of
filling to within ½ inch of filling. Fold strips alternately over filling from each side, overlapping at an
angle. Cover and let rise in a warm place, free from
drafts, 1 hour or until doubled in bulk.

Uncover dough. Brush with egg white; sprinkle
with almonds and 1 tablespoon sugar. Bake at 350°
for 30 minutes or until loaf sounds hollow when
tapped. Cool loaf on wire rack. Yield: 1 loaf,
16 (1-inch) slices.

PER SLICE: 218 CALORIES (12% FROM FAT)
FAT 2.8G (SATURATED FAT 0.6G)
PROTEIN 6.2G   CARBOHYDRATE 41.7G
CHOLESTEROL 1MG   SODIUM 103MG

RASPBERRY-PECAN TEA RING

Tender Yeast Bread dough (page 58)
1 (10-ounce) package frozen raspberries in
   light syrup, thawed
¼ cup plus 2 tablespoons firmly packed brown
   sugar
2 tablespoons plus 2 teaspoons cornstarch
½ cup finely chopped pecans, toasted
Vegetable cooking spray
¼ cup plus 2 tablespoons sifted powdered
   sugar
1½ teaspoons skim milk
¼ teaspoon vanilla extract

Spread raspberry filling over dough; sprinkle with pecans. Starting with long side, roll dough up tightly; pinch seam to seal.

   Prepare dough for Tender Yeast Bread. After first
rising, punch dough down; turn out onto a lightly
floured surface. Cover and let rest 10 minutes.
   Press raspberries through a sieve, reserving ¾
cup plus 2 tablespoons juice; discard seeds.
Combine reserved juice, brown sugar, and cornstarch in a small saucepan; stir well. Bring to a boil,
and cook, stirring constantly, 1 minute. Pour into a
bowl; cool.
   Divide dough in half; roll each portion into an
18- x 12-inch rectangle on a lightly floured surface.
Spread raspberry filling evenly over portions of
dough, leaving a ½-inch margin around edges.
Sprinkle dough evenly with pecans. Roll up halves
tightly, starting at long side; pinch seam to seal.
Place each roll, seam side down, on a baking sheet
coated with cooking spray; bring ends together to
form a ring. Pinch ends together to seal. Using
kitchen shears, cut slits 1 inch apart around outside
edge to within ½ inch of center. Cover and let rise
in a warm place (85°), free from drafts, 45 minutes
or until doubled in bulk.

Form dough into a ring, pinching ends together to seal. Using kitchen shears, cut slits 1 inch apart around outside edge to within ½ inch of center.

   Uncover and bake at 350° for 20 minutes or until
rings sound hollow when tapped. Cool on wire
racks. Combine powdered sugar, milk, and vanilla
in a bowl; stir well. Drizzle over tea rings. Yield:
2 tea rings, 18 slices each.

PER SLICE: 149 CALORIES (19% FROM FAT)
FAT 3.2G (SATURATED FAT 0.5G)
PROTEIN 3.9G   CARBOHYDRATE 26.3G
CHOLESTEROL 6MG   SODIUM 110MG

Combine powdered sugar, milk, and vanilla; drizzle tea rings with glaze.

Chocolate-Mocha Torte (recipe on page 84)

ALL-OCCASION CAKES

*W*hether it's a birthday party, covered-dish supper, or anniversary dinner, Ultimate Chocolate Layer Cake (page 83) will be perfect for the occasion. Its luscious chocolate layers filled and topped with a rich chocolate icing make it hard to imagine that it could be low in fat!

This chapter is bursting with a variety of cake and cupcake recipes for all ages. If you're trying to please the younger set, bake a batch of Chocolate Cream Cupcakes (page 76). When adult friends are your guests, treat them to Chocolate Roulade (page 90). Young and old alike should enjoy Pineapple Upside-Down Cake (page 81) or Sour Cream-Lemon Pound Cake (page 87).

These recipes take the guesswork out of baking with low-fat ingredients. All you need to do is pay attention to the recommended amounts and techniques. Turn to page 76 for specific guidelines.

CHOCOLATE-COCONUT CUPCAKES

3 tablespoons unsweetened cocoa
1 teaspoon ground cinnamon
½ cup boiling water
⅔ cup plain nonfat yogurt
1 teaspoon baking soda
½ cup sugar
2 tablespoons stick margarine, melted
1 egg yolk
1 cup all-purpose flour
3 tablespoons shredded sweetened coconut
1 teaspoon vanilla extract
½ teaspoon almond extract
¼ teaspoon salt
1 egg white
1½ tablespoons water
1 teaspoon stick margarine
½ ounce semisweet chocolate, chopped
1 cup sifted powdered sugar
½ teaspoon ground cinnamon
½ teaspoon vanilla extract

Combine cocoa and 1 teaspoon cinnamon in a small bowl. Add boiling water, stirring until cocoa dissolves. Combine yogurt and baking soda.

Combine ½ cup sugar, 2 tablespoons margarine, and egg yolk. Beat at high speed of an electric mixer 1 minute. Add cocoa mixture, yogurt mixture, flour, and next 3 ingredients; mix well.

Beat salt and egg white with clean beaters at high speed until stiff peaks form. Fold into batter; spoon batter evenly into muffin cups lined with paper liners. Bake at 350° for 20 minutes or until cupcakes spring back when touched lightly in center.

Combine 1½ tablespoons water, 1 teaspoon margarine, and chocolate in a small saucepan. Place over medium-low heat until chocolate melts. Remove from heat; stir in powdered sugar, ½ teaspoon cinnamon, and ½ teaspoon vanilla. Spread 2 teaspoons glaze over each warm cupcake. Cool on wire racks. Yield: 1 dozen.

PER CUPCAKE: 164 CALORIES (21% FROM FAT)
FAT 3.9G (SATURATED FAT 1.4G)
PROTEIN 2.9G   CARBOHYDRATE 29.6G
CHOLESTEROL 18MG   SODIUM 199MG

CHOCOLATE CREAM CUPCAKES

1 (20.5-ounce) package low-fat fudge brownie mix
⅔ cup water
Vegetable cooking spray
½ (8-ounce) block ⅓-less-fat cream cheese
3 tablespoons sugar
1 teaspoon fat-free egg substitute
2 tablespoons semisweet chocolate morsels, melted

Combine brownie mix and water; stir until blended. Spoon into muffin cups lined with paper liners coated with cooking spray.

Combine cheese and sugar, beating at medium speed of an electric mixer until light and fluffy. Add egg substitute, beating well. Stir in melted chocolate. Spoon 2 heaping teaspoons cheese mixture into center of each cupcake. Bake at 350° for 25 minutes or until centers are set. Remove from pan, and cool on a wire rack. Yield: 1 dozen.

PER CUPCAKE: 256 CALORIES (24% FROM FAT)
FAT 6.7G (SATURATED FAT 2.5G)
PROTEIN 4.1G   CARBOHYDRATE 44.9G
CHOLESTEROL 7MG   SODIUM 203MG

Steps to Success

Follow these tips for making perfect cakes and cupcakes.

• Position oven rack in center of oven; preheat oven.

• Use the type of flour specified; sift if indicated. Measure accurately. (See pages 7 through 10 for more about using flour.)

• Let margarine and milk reach room temperature before mixing.

• When indicated, beat margarine and sugar well at the beginning of the mixing process.

• Test for doneness before removing cake from oven. Underbaking can cause a cake to fall.

Chocolate Cream Cupcakes

Blackberry Jam Cake

BLACKBERRY JAM CAKE

Vegetable cooking spray
1 cup plus 2 teaspoons sifted cake flour, divided
½ cup 1% low-fat milk
1 tablespoon stick margarine
2 eggs, separated
½ cup sugar
1 teaspoon baking powder
⅛ teaspoon salt
1 teaspoon vanilla extract
1 teaspoon almond extract
½ cup seedless blackberry jam
2 teaspoons powdered sugar

Coat an 8-inch round cakepan with cooking spray; dust with 2 teaspoons flour, and set aside.

Heat milk and margarine in a heavy saucepan over medium-high heat to 180°. (Do not boil.) Remove from heat; set aside.

Beat egg whites at high speed of an electric mixer until foamy. Add ½ cup sugar, 1 tablespoon at a time, beating until stiff peaks form. Add egg yolks; beat mixture well. Combine remaining 1 cup flour, baking powder, and salt; add to egg white mixture alternately with milk mixture, beginning and ending with flour mixture. Beat at low speed after each addition. Stir in flavorings. (Batter will be thin.)

Pour batter into prepared pan. Bake at 350° for 20 to 25 minutes or until a wooden pick inserted in center comes out clean. Cool in pan 10 minutes on a wire rack; remove from pan. Cool on wire rack.

Using a serrated knife, split cake in half horizontally; place bottom layer, cut side up, on a serving plate. Spread with jam; top with remaining layer, cut side down. Place a paper doily on top; sift powdered sugar over doily. Remove doily. Yield: 8 servings.

PER SERVING: 196 CALORIES (14% FROM FAT)
FAT 3.1G (SATURATED FAT 0.8G)
PROTEIN 3.3G   CARBOHYDRATE 38.5G
CHOLESTEROL 56MG   SODIUM 118MG

BLUEBERRY STREUSEL CAKE

1½ cups fresh or frozen blueberries, thawed
    and drained
¼ cup sugar
⅓ cup vanilla wafer crumbs (about 8 cookies)
¼ cup firmly packed brown sugar
1 tablespoon stick margarine, melted
1 teaspoon hot water
1½ cups all-purpose flour
¾ teaspoon baking powder
¼ teaspoon baking soda
⅛ teaspoon salt
⅓ cup sugar
¾ cup plain low-fat yogurt
3 tablespoons vegetable oil
1 teaspoon vanilla extract
1 egg
1 egg white
Vegetable cooking spray

Combine blueberries and ¼ cup sugar; gently mash with a potato masher until blueberries are crushed. Let stand 5 minutes. Set aside.

Combine wafer crumbs and next 3 ingredients; stir until well blended. Set aside.

Combine flour and next 4 ingredients in a large bowl. Combine yogurt and next 4 ingredients; stir well with a wire whisk. Add to flour mixture, stirring until well blended. Fold in blueberry mixture.

Pour batter into a 9-inch round cakepan coated with cooking spray. Bake at 350° for 30 minutes. Sprinkle brown sugar mixture over cake; bake 10 additional minutes or until a wooden pick inserted in center comes out clean. Cool in pan on a wire rack. Yield: 8 servings.

PER SERVING: 287 CALORIES (28% FROM FAT)
FAT 8.8G (SATURATED FAT 2.3G)
PROTEIN 5.2G CARBOHYDRATE 47.3G
CHOLESTEROL 33MG SODIUM 180MG

LEMON GINGERBREAD CAKE

2 tablespoons sugar
2 tablespoons stick margarine, softened
2 teaspoons grated lemon rind
1 egg white
½ cup nonfat buttermilk
½ cup molasses
1 cup all-purpose flour
½ cup whole wheat flour
½ teaspoon baking soda
¼ teaspoon salt
¼ teaspoon ground ginger
¼ teaspoon ground cinnamon
Vegetable cooking spray
2 teaspoons powdered sugar

Beat sugar and margarine at medium speed of an electric mixer until light and fluffy (about 5 minutes). Add lemon rind and egg white; beat at medium speed until well blended.

Combine buttermilk and molasses; set aside. Combine all-purpose flour and next 5 ingredients. Add flour mixture to creamed mixture alternately with buttermilk mixture, beginning and ending with flour mixture. Beat at low speed after each addition until blended.

Pour batter into an 8-inch square baking pan coated with cooking spray. Bake at 350° for 25 minutes or until a wooden pick inserted in center comes out clean. Cool completely in pan on a wire rack; sprinkle with powdered sugar. To serve, cut into squares. Yield: 9 servings.

PER SERVING: 159 CALORIES (16% FROM FAT)
FAT 2.9G (SATURATED FAT 0.6G)
PROTEIN 3.2G CARBOHYDRATE 30.6G
CHOLESTEROL 0MG SODIUM 168MG

MIDWESTERN OATMEAL CAKE

1 cup boiling water
1 cup quick-cooking oats, uncooked and divided
2 eggs
1 cup plus 2 tablespoons firmly packed brown
    sugar, divided
⅓ cup unsweetened applesauce
1½ teaspoons vanilla extract
1¼ cups all-purpose flour
½ teaspoon baking powder
½ teaspoon baking soda
¼ teaspoon salt
1 teaspoon ground cinnamon
Vegetable cooking spray
¼ cup evaporated skimmed milk
1½ tablespoons stick margarine
¼ cup shredded coconut
¼ cup chopped pecans

Combine boiling water and ¾ cup oats; stir well, and set aside.

Beat eggs in a large bowl at medium speed of an electric mixer until thick and pale (about 4 minutes). Gradually add ¾ cup plus 2 tablespoons brown sugar, applesauce, and vanilla, beating constantly. Add oats mixture; beat well.

Combine flour and next 4 ingredients; stir well. Add flour mixture to oats mixture, beating at low speed until blended.

Pour batter into a 9-inch round cakepan coated with cooking spray. Bake at 350° for 45 minutes or until a wooden pick inserted in center comes out clean; cool in pan on a wire rack.

Combine milk and margarine in a saucepan; cook over medium-low heat until margarine melts. Add remaining ¼ cup brown sugar; cook until dissolved, stirring constantly. Add remaining ¼ cup oats, coconut, and pecans; cook, stirring constantly, 4 minutes or until thickened. Spread over cake; broil 3 inches from heat (with electric oven door partially opened) 3 minutes or until golden. Cool. Yield: 10 servings.

PER SERVING: 250 CALORIES (23% FROM FAT)
FAT 6.3G (SATURATED FAT 1.7G)
PROTEIN 4.8G CARBOHYDRATE 44.2G
CHOLESTEROL 43MG SODIUM 114MG

APRICOT UPSIDE-DOWN CAKE

1¼ cups unsweetened pineapple juice
¾ cup dried apricots, quartered
2 tablespoons stick margarine
⅓ cup firmly packed dark brown sugar
2 tablespoons finely chopped walnuts
¾ cup all-purpose flour
1 teaspoon baking powder
½ cup sugar, divided
⅓ cup 1% low-fat milk
1 egg yolk
1 teaspoon vanilla extract
3 egg whites

Combine pineapple juice and apricots in a small saucepan; bring to a boil. Reduce heat; simmer 8 minutes or until apricots are plump. Drain apricots in a colander over a bowl, reserving ⅓ cup juice.

Melt margarine in a 9-inch cast-iron skillet over medium heat. Spoon 1 tablespoon melted margarine into a small bowl; set aside. Add reserved pineapple juice and brown sugar to margarine in skillet. Bring to a boil; cook 1 minute or until slightly thickened. Sprinkle apricots and walnuts over brown sugar mixture; set aside.

Combine flour and baking powder in a large bowl. Add ¼ cup sugar and next 3 ingredients, stirring well. Add to flour mixture, stirring well; set aside.

Beat egg whites at high speed of an electric mixer until foamy. Gradually add remaining ¼ cup sugar, 1 tablespoon at a time, beating until stiff peaks almost form. Gently stir one-fourth of egg white mixture into batter; gently fold in remaining egg white mixture. Pour batter over apricot mixture in skillet.

Bake at 350° for 30 minutes or until a wooden pick inserted in center comes out clean. Let stand 5 minutes on a wire rack. Loosen cake from sides of skillet, using a narrow metal spatula. Invert onto a serving platter; cut into wedges. Yield: 8 servings.

PER SERVING: 210 CALORIES (21% FROM FAT)
FAT 4.9G (SATURATED FAT 0.9G)
PROTEIN 4.2G CARBOHYDRATE 38.5G
CHOLESTEROL 28MG SODIUM 114MG

PINEAPPLE UPSIDE-DOWN CAKE

*A cast-iron skillet works best for making the cake golden and crispy on
the outside and tender on the inside.*

⅓ cup reduced-calorie stick margarine
¾ cup firmly packed brown sugar
⅓ cup chopped pecans
1 (15¼-ounce) can sliced pineapple in juice
½ (18.25-ounce) package reduced-fat yellow
   cake mix
¼ cup plus 2 tablespoons fat-free egg
   substitute
⅓ cup water
7 maraschino cherries with stems

Melt margarine in a 10-inch cast-iron skillet over
low heat. Set aside 1 tablespoon melted margarine.
Add sugar and pecans to margarine in skillet, stirring well. Drain pineapple, reserving ⅓ cup juice.

Reserve remaining juice for another use. Arrange
pineapple slices over sugar mixture.

Combine reserved 1 tablespoon margarine, ⅓
cup juice, cake mix, egg substitute, and water. Beat
at low speed of an electric mixer 30 seconds. Beat
at medium speed 2 minutes.

Pour batter over pineapple in skillet. Bake at
350° for 35 minutes or until a wooden pick inserted
in center comes out clean. Immediately invert cake
onto a serving platter. Place cherries in centers of
pineapple rings. Yield: 10 servings.

PER SERVING: 254 CALORIES (28% FROM FAT)
FAT 8.0G (SATURATED FAT 1.5G)
PROTEIN 2.3G   CARBOHYDRATE 44.5G
CHOLESTEROL 0MG   SODIUM 244MG

Pineapple Upside-Down Cake

Mocha Pudding Cake

MOCHA PUDDING CAKE

1 cup all-purpose flour
2 teaspoons baking powder
¼ teaspoon salt
1 cup sugar, divided
¼ cup plus 2 tablespoons unsweetened cocoa, divided
1½ tablespoons instant coffee granules
½ cup 1% low-fat milk
3 tablespoons vegetable oil
1 teaspoon vanilla extract
Vegetable cooking spray
1 cup boiling water
2¼ cups low-fat vanilla ice cream

Combine flour, baking powder, salt, ⅔ cup sugar, ¼ cup cocoa, and coffee granules in a large bowl.

Combine milk, oil, and vanilla; add to flour mixture, stirring well. Pour batter into an 8-inch square pan coated with cooking spray.

Combine remaining ⅓ cup sugar and remaining 2 tablespoons cocoa. Sprinkle over batter. Pour boiling water evenly over batter. (Do not stir.) Bake at 350° for 30 minutes or until cake springs back when touched lightly in center. Serve cake warm, topped with ice cream (¼ cup per serving). Yield: 9 servings.

PER SERVING: 247 CALORIES (25% FROM FAT)
FAT 6.8G (SATURATED FAT 2.1G)
PROTEIN 4.2G CARBOHYDRATE 43.0G
CHOLESTEROL 5MG SODIUM 191MG

ULTIMATE CHOCOLATE LAYER CAKE

Vegetable cooking spray
2 cups sugar
½ cup plus 2 tablespoons light stick butter, softened
¾ cup fat-free egg substitute
2 cups all-purpose flour
¾ teaspoon baking soda
¼ teaspoon salt
½ cup unsweetened cocoa
¾ cup low-fat sour cream
¾ cup boiling water
1 teaspoon vanilla extract
Chocolate Frosting

Coat bottoms of two 8-inch round cakepans with cooking spray (do not coat sides of pan); line bottoms of pans with wax paper. Coat wax paper with cooking spray; set aside.

Beat sugar and butter at medium speed of an electric mixer until well blended. Gradually add egg substitute; beat well. Combine flour and next 3 ingredients; add to sugar mixture alternately with sour cream, beginning and ending with flour mixture. Mix at low speed after each addition until blended. Gently stir in boiling water and vanilla.

Pour batter into prepared pans. Bake at 350° for 35 minutes or until cake springs back when touched lightly in center. Loosen layers from sides of pans, using a narrow metal spatula; turn out onto wire racks. Peel off wax paper; cool.

Place 1 cake layer on a plate, and spread with ½ cup Chocolate Frosting. Top with other layer; spread remaining Chocolate Frosting over cake. Yield: 18 servings.

CHOCOLATE FROSTING

4 ounces tub-style light cream cheese, softened
3 tablespoons skim milk
3 (1-ounce) squares semisweet chocolate, melted
3 cups sifted powdered sugar
¼ cup unsweetened cocoa
1 teaspoon vanilla extract

Beat cream cheese and milk at high speed of an electric mixer until creamy. Add melted chocolate, and beat until well blended.

Combine sugar and cocoa; gradually add to cream cheese mixture, beating at low speed until well blended. Add vanilla, and beat well 1 minute until creamy. Yield: 1¾ cups.

Note: Make this frosting right before spreading it on the cake—otherwise, it will dry out.

PER SERVING: 315 CALORIES (22% FROM FAT)
FAT 7.8G (SATURATED FAT 4.9G)
PROTEIN 4.8G CARBOHYDRATE 58.4G
CHOLESTEROL 19MG SODIUM 129MG

Ultimate Chocolate Layer Cake

CHOCOLATE-MOCHA TORTE

(pictured on page 74)

1 (18-ounce) package low-fat devil's food cake
   mix
1¾ cups water
4 egg whites
Vegetable cooking spray
½ cup semisweet chocolate morsels
2 teaspoons instant espresso powder
½ cup plain nonfat yogurt
½ cup nonfat cottage cheese
1 tablespoon vanilla extract
2 teaspoons powdered sugar
3 tablespoons grated semisweet chocolate
Fresh strawberry halves (optional)

Combine first 3 ingredients in a mixing bowl. Beat
at medium speed of an electric mixer 30 seconds.
Beat 2 minutes at high speed. Pour batter into two
8-inch round cakepans coated with cooking spray.
Bake at 350° for 25 minutes or until a wooden pick
inserted in center comes out clean. Cool in pans on
wire racks 10 minutes; remove from pans, and cool
on wire racks. Slice each cake layer in half horizontally. (Keep layers covered to prevent drying.)

Place chocolate morsels in top of a double boiler;
bring water to a boil. Reduce heat to low; cook
until chocolate melts. Remove from heat, and stir
in espresso powder. Set aside, and keep warm.

Combine yogurt and cottage cheese in container
of an electric blender; cover and process until
smooth. Transfer to a small bowl. Gradually add
chocolate mixture to yogurt mixture, stirring with a
wire whisk until combined. Stir in vanilla.

Place 1 cake layer on a serving plate; spread with
one-third of chocolate mixture. Repeat layers twice;
top with remaining cake layer.

Cover and chill at least 2 hours. Sprinkle powdered
sugar and grated chocolate in a checkerboard design
over cake just before serving. Garnish with strawberry halves, if desired. Yield: 12 servings.

PER SERVING: 221 CALORIES (28% FROM FAT)
FAT 6.8G (SATURATED FAT 2.5G)
PROTEIN 5.3G CARBOHYDRATE 39.0G
CHOLESTEROL 1MG SODIUM 400MG

*Cut 1½-inch-wide strips of aluminum foil;
place over powdered sugar-topped cake in
a checkerboard design.*

*Sprinkle finely grated chocolate over cake,
covering the visible powdered sugar.*

*Carefully remove foil strips, leaving a
checkerboard design over top of cake.*

CHOCOLATE POTATO CAKE

A 9- x 5- x 3-inch loafpan is a suitable substitute for the Bundt pan. Bake at 325° for 45 to 50 minutes.

Vegetable cooking spray
1 cup plus 1 tablespoon sifted cake flour, divided
1 medium-size baking potato, peeled and cut into 1½-inch pieces (about 6 ounces)
¾ cup boiling water
½ cup firmly packed dark brown sugar
½ cup light-colored corn syrup
¼ cup shortening
1 egg
1 teaspoon baking powder
½ teaspoon baking soda
¼ teaspoon salt
½ cup unsweetened cocoa
1 tablespoon powdered sugar

Coat a 6-cup Bundt pan with cooking spray; dust with 1 tablespoon flour, and set aside.

Place potato in a saucepan; cover with water, and bring to a boil. Reduce heat, and simmer, uncovered, 15 minutes or until potato is very tender; drain. Press potato through a sieve into a bowl. Spoon ½ cup potato into a bowl; discard remaining potato. Add ¾ cup boiling water to potato, stirring until smooth; set aside.

Combine brown sugar, corn syrup, and shortening in a large bowl; beat at medium speed of an electric mixer 5 minutes. Add egg; beat well.

Sift together remaining 1 cup flour, baking powder, and next 3 ingredients; add to creamed mixture alternately with potato mixture, beginning and ending with flour mixture. Mix at low speed after each addition until blended.

Pour batter into prepared pan. Bake at 325° for 40 minutes or until cake springs back when touched lightly in center. Cool 10 minutes; remove from pan, and cool completely on a wire rack. Sprinkle with powdered sugar. Yield: 12 servings.

PER SERVING: 174 CALORIES (24% FROM FAT)
FAT 4.6G (SATURATED FAT 1.5G)
PROTEIN 2.6G   CARBOHYDRATE 30.8G
CHOLESTEROL 19MG   SODIUM 135MG

RUM-GLAZED BANANA CAKE

1¾ cups firmly packed brown sugar
⅔ cup stick margarine, softened
¾ cup fat-free egg substitute
1 cup mashed ripe banana
½ cup vanilla low-fat yogurt
1 tablespoon vanilla extract
2½ cups all-purpose flour
2 teaspoons baking powder
1 teaspoon baking soda
1 teaspoon ground cinnamon
Vegetable cooking spray
¾ cup sifted powdered sugar
2 tablespoons dark rum or ¼ teaspoon imitation rum extract
1 tablespoon stick margarine, melted

Beat brown sugar and ⅔ cup margarine at medium speed of an electric mixer until light and fluffy. Add egg substitute, beating mixture until well blended.

Combine banana, yogurt, and vanilla. Combine flour and next 3 ingredients; add to sugar mixture alternately with banana mixture, beginning and ending with flour mixture. Mix at low speed after each addition until blended.

Pour batter into a 10-inch tube pan coated with cooking spray. Bake at 375° for 1 hour or until a wooden pick inserted in center comes out clean. Cool in pan 10 minutes; remove from pan. Cool completely on a wire rack.

Combine powdered sugar, rum, and melted margarine; stir until smooth. Drizzle over cake. Yield: 16 servings.

PER SERVING: 285 CALORIES (27% FROM FAT)
FAT 8.7G (SATURATED FAT 1.7G)
PROTEIN 3.6G   CARBOHYDRATE 47.5G
CHOLESTEROL 0MG   SODIUM 230MG

Cornmeal Pound Cake with Orange Sauce

CORNMEAL POUND CAKE WITH ORANGE SAUCE

3 large navel oranges (about 1¾ pounds)
1½ cups sifted powdered sugar
1¼ cups sifted cake flour
1 teaspoon baking powder
½ teaspoon salt
½ cup yellow cornmeal
2 eggs, lightly beaten
½ cup plain nonfat yogurt
¼ cup vegetable oil
1 teaspoon vanilla extract
Vegetable cooking spray
2 cups unsweetened orange juice
1¼ cups sugar
3 whole cloves
Orange rind strips (optional)

Grate 1 tablespoon rind from oranges. Peel oranges; cut each orange in half lengthwise. Cut each half crosswise into thin slices to make 2 cups; set aside.

Combine 1 tablespoon orange rind, powdered sugar, and next 4 ingredients in a large bowl; stir well. Combine eggs and next 3 ingredients, stirring mixture well. Add to flour mixture; beat at medium speed of an electric mixer 1 minute or until smooth.

Pour batter into an 8½- x 4½- x 3-inch loafpan coated with cooking spray. Bake at 325° for 50 minutes or until a wooden pick inserted in center comes out clean. Cool in pan on a wire rack 5 minutes; remove from pan, and cool on a wire rack.

Combine orange juice, 1¼ cups sugar, and cloves in a medium saucepan. Bring to a boil over medium heat; cook 25 minutes or until reduced to 1½ cups, stirring occasionally. Remove from heat; stir in reserved 2 cups orange slices. Serve warm or at room temperature over slices of cake (3 tablespoons of sauce per serving). Garnish with orange rind strips, if desired. Yield: 14 servings.

PER SERVING: 247 CALORIES (18% FROM FAT)
FAT 4.9G (SATURATED FAT 1.0G)
PROTEIN 3.0G CARBOHYDRATE 48.9G
CHOLESTEROL 31MG SODIUM 121MG

SOUR CREAM-LEMON POUND CAKE

(pictured on cover)

⅔ cup stick margarine, softened
2⅔ cups sugar
1¼ cups fat-free egg substitute
1½ cups low-fat sour cream
1 teaspoon baking soda
4½ cups sifted cake flour
¼ teaspoon salt
2 teaspoons vanilla extract
Vegetable cooking spray
½ cup sifted powdered sugar
1 teaspoon grated lemon rind
1 tablespoon fresh lemon juice
Lemon slices (optional)
Lemon rind curls (optional)

Beat margarine at medium speed of an electric mixer until creamy; gradually add 2⅔ cups sugar, beating well. Add egg substitute, and beat well.

Combine sour cream and soda, stirring well. Combine flour and salt; add to margarine mixture alternately with sour cream mixture, beginning and ending with flour mixture. Mix at low speed after each addition until blended. Stir in vanilla.

Pour batter into a 10-inch tube pan coated with cooking spray. Bake at 325° for 1 hour and 20 minutes or until a wooden pick inserted in center comes out clean. Cool in pan 10 minutes.

Remove cake from pan. Combine powdered sugar, grated lemon rind, and lemon juice; drizzle over cake. Cool completely on a wire rack. If desired, garnish with lemon slices and lemon rind curls. Yield: 24 servings.

PER SERVING: 242 CALORIES (26% FROM FAT)
FAT 7.0G (SATURATED FAT 2.1G)
PROTEIN 3.4G CARBOHYDRATE 41.7G
CHOLESTEROL 6MG SODIUM 161MG

PUMPKIN-PECAN POUND CAKE

Pumpkin adds flavor and moistness to this cake; it's also a significant source of beta carotene, an antioxidant that may help fight disease.

¾ cup stick margarine, softened
1½ cups firmly packed brown sugar
1 cup sugar
1¼ cups fat-free egg substitute
1 (16-ounce) can pumpkin
⅓ cup bourbon
3 cups all-purpose flour
2 teaspoons baking powder
½ teaspoon baking soda
¼ teaspoon salt
2 teaspoons pumpkin pie spice
¼ cup chopped pecans
Vegetable cooking spray

Beat margarine at medium speed of an electric mixer until creamy; gradually add sugars, beating well. Add egg substitute, and beat well.

Combine pumpkin and bourbon, stirring well. Combine flour and next 4 ingredients; add to margarine mixture alternately with pumpkin mixture, beginning and ending with flour mixture. Mix at low speed after each addition until blended.

Sprinkle pecans in a 10-inch tube pan coated with cooking spray. Pour batter over pecans. Bake at 325° for 1 hour and 35 minutes or until a wooden pick inserted in center comes out clean. Cool in pan 10 minutes. Remove cake from pan; cool completely on a wire rack. Yield: 24 servings.

PER SERVING: 213 CALORIES (28% FROM FAT)
FAT 6.7G (SATURATED FAT 1.2G)
PROTEIN 3.2G CARBOHYDRATE 35.7G
CHOLESTEROL 0MG SODIUM 176MG

SWEET POTATO CAKE

*This cake is so moist that it doesn't
need a frosting or glaze.*

2 cups sugar
¾ cup stick margarine, softened
¾ cup fat-free egg substitute
2 (14½-ounce) cans unsweetened mashed
   sweet potatoes
3 cups sifted cake flour
1 teaspoon baking powder
1 teaspoon baking soda
½ teaspoon salt
1½ teaspoons ground cinnamon
½ teaspoon ground nutmeg
2 teaspoons vanilla extract
Vegetable cooking spray
¼ cup flaked sweetened coconut
2 tablespoons finely chopped pecans

Beat sugar and margarine at medium speed of
an electric mixer until well blended (about 5 minutes). Gradually add egg substitute, beating well.
Add 2½ cups sweet potatoes (about 1½ cans); beat
well. Reserve remaining potatoes for another use.

Combine flour and next 5 ingredients; stir well.
Gradually add flour mixture to sweet potato mixture, beating well after each addition. Stir in
vanilla.

Pour batter into a 10-inch tube pan coated with
cooking spray. Sprinkle coconut and pecans over
batter. Bake at 350° for 1 hour and 25 minutes or
until a wooden pick inserted in center comes out
clean. Cool in pan 10 minutes; remove from pan.
Cool completely on a wire rack. Yield: 16 servings.

Note: Substitute 6 egg whites (about ¾ cup) for
egg substitute, if desired.

PER SERVING: 298 CALORIES (30% FROM FAT)
FAT 10.0G (SATURATED FAT 2.3G)
PROTEIN 3.6G   CARBOHYDRATE 50.7G
CHOLESTEROL 0MG   SODIUM 286MG

BASIC SPONGE CAKE

*Here's a basic recipe that can play double-duty:
make it as a simple sponge cake, or use it
as the basis for Sugared Almond-Topped Cake
on the facing page.*

1 cup sifted cake flour
1 teaspoon baking powder
¼ teaspoon salt
3 eggs, separated
1 cup sugar, divided
2 teaspoons vanilla extract
¼ cup water
2 egg whites

Combine first 3 ingredients; stir well, and set
aside. Beat 3 egg yolks in a large mixing bowl at
high speed of an electric mixer 1 minute. Gradually
add ¾ cup sugar, beating constantly until egg yolks
are thick and pale (about 5 minutes). Add vanilla
and ¼ cup water, beating at low speed until
blended. Add flour mixture to egg yolk mixture,
beating at low speed until blended; set aside.

Beat 5 egg whites in a large bowl with clean
beaters at high speed of mixer until foamy. Gradually add remaining ¼ cup sugar, 1 tablespoon at
a time, beating until stiff peaks form (see page 90).
Gently stir one-fourth of egg white mixture into
batter; gently fold in remaining egg white mixture.

Pour batter into an ungreased 10-inch tube pan.
Bake at 350° for 35 minutes or until cake springs
back when touched lightly in center. Invert pan;
cool 45 minutes.

Loosen cake from sides of pan, using a narrow
metal spatula; remove cake from pan. Cool completely on a wire rack. Yield: 10 servings.

PER SERVING: 141 CALORIES (10% FROM FAT)
FAT 1.6G (SATURATED FAT 0.5G)
PROTEIN 3.4G   CARBOHYDRATE 28.0G
CHOLESTEROL 64MG   SODIUM 119MG

SUGARED ALMOND-TOPPED CAKE

If you want a stronger almond flavor in this cake, substitute 1 teaspoon almond extract for the 2 teaspoons vanilla extract in the recipe for Basic Sponge Cake.

Basic Sponge Cake batter (facing page)
⅓ cup firmly packed brown sugar
2 tablespoons all-purpose flour
¼ teaspoon ground cinnamon
2 tablespoons stick margarine
1 tablespoon plus 1 teaspoon skim milk
⅓ cup sliced almonds

Pour Basic Sponge Cake batter into an ungreased 10-inch springform pan, spreading batter evenly. Bake at 350° for 25 minutes or until cake springs back when touched lightly in center.

Combine sugar, flour, and cinnamon; stir well. Melt margarine in a small saucepan over medium heat; add sugar mixture, stirring well. Gradually add milk, stirring with a wire whisk. Cook, stirring constantly, 2 minutes. Remove from heat; stir in almonds. Spread almond mixture over warm cake.

Broil cake 3 inches from heat (with electric oven door partially opened) 1 minute or until bubbly. Using a sharp knife, cut into wedges. Serve warm or at room temperature. Yield: 10 servings.

PER SERVING: 214 CALORIES (24% FROM FAT)
FAT 5.6G (SATURATED FAT 1.1G)
PROTEIN 4.2G   CARBOHYDRATE 37.0G
CHOLESTEROL 64MG   SODIUM 149MG

Sugared Almond-Topped Cake

CHOCOLATE ROULADE

Vegetable cooking spray
2 tablespoons fine, dry breadcrumbs
4 large egg yolks
¾ cup sugar, divided
6 large egg whites
⅛ teaspoon salt
1 teaspoon vanilla extract
½ cup Dutch process cocoa
2 tablespoons powdered sugar
2 cups frozen reduced-calorie whipped
     topping, thawed
3 tablespoons plus 1 teaspoon chocolate syrup
2½ cups raspberries

Coat a 15- x 10- x 1-inch jellyroll pan with cooking spray; line with wax paper. Coat wax paper with cooking spray. Dust with breadcrumbs; set aside.

Beat egg yolks in a bowl at high speed of an electric mixer 4 minutes. Add ¼ cup sugar, beating until thick and pale (about 2 minutes). Beat egg whites in a large bowl with clean beaters at high speed until foamy; add salt. Add remaining ½ cup sugar, 1 tablespoon at a time, beating until stiff peaks form. Stir in vanilla. Gradually add cocoa; stir until well blended. Gently stir one-fourth of egg white mixture into egg yolk mixture; gently fold in remaining egg white mixture.

Pour batter into prepared pan, spreading to sides of pan. Bake at 375° for 15 minutes or until cake springs back when touched lightly in center. Loosen cake from sides of pan; turn out onto a cloth towel dusted with powdered sugar, and carefully peel off wax paper. Cool 1 minute. Starting at narrow end, roll up cake and towel together. Place, seam side down, on a wire rack; cool completely (about 1 hour).

Unroll cake carefully; remove towel. Spread whipped topping over cake, leaving a ½-inch margin around outside edges. Reroll cake; place, seam side down, on a platter. Cover; chill 1 hour. Cut into slices. Drizzle syrup evenly on 10 plates. Place a slice on each plate; top evenly with raspberries. Yield: 10 servings.

PER SERVING: 181 CALORIES (24% FROM FAT)
FAT 4.8G (SATURATED FAT 2.2G)
PROTEIN 5.4G CARBOHYDRATE 29.5G
CHOLESTEROL 87MG SODIUM 91MG

PERFECT EGG WHITES

Let egg whites stand at room temperature 20 minutes. Add cream of tartar (in some recipes); beat at high speed until foamy.

Add sugar as directed. At soft-peak stage, the egg whites will gently fold over when beaters are pulled away.

When glossy peaks form, the egg whites are stiff. At this stage, they will stand up when the beaters are pulled away.

Devilish Angel Food Cake

DEVILISH ANGEL FOOD CAKE

⅔ cup sifted cake flour
⅓ cup unsweetened cocoa
¼ cup sugar
½ teaspoon ground cinnamon
12 large egg whites
1 teaspoon cream of tartar
2 teaspoons warm water
1 teaspoon vanilla extract
½ teaspoon salt
1 cup sugar

Sift together first 4 ingredients in a large bowl, and set aside.

Beat egg whites and next 4 ingredients in a large bowl at high speed of an electric mixer until foamy. Gradually add 1 cup sugar, 2 tablespoons at a time, beating until stiff peaks form (see page 90). Sift flour mixture over egg white mixture, ¼ cup at a time, and fold flour mixture in gently.

Spoon batter into an ungreased 10-inch tube pan, spreading evenly. Break air pockets by cutting through batter with a knife. Bake at 350° for 45 minutes or until cake springs back when touched lightly in center. Invert pan; cool completely. Loosen cake from sides of pan, using a narrow spatula; invert cake onto plate. Yield: 8 servings.

PER SERVING: 196 CALORIES (3% FROM FAT)
FAT 0.6G (SATURATED FAT 0.3G)
PROTEIN 6.9G   CARBOHYDRATE 41.0G
CHOLESTEROL 0MG   SODIUM 227MG

Strawberry-Oat Squares (recipe on page 109)

COOKIES & BARS

*T*he next time you get caught with your hand in the cookie jar, don't feel guilty. These homemade treats are lower in fat and calories than regular cookies. So enjoy indulging in White Chocolate Chip Cookies (page 96), traditional Cinnamon Sugar Cookies (page 99), or even chewy Easy Chocolate-Caramel Brownies (page 104).

A few key changes were critical in cutting the fat from these recipes while keeping old-fashioned taste. Each recipe calls for a minimal amount of fat and is specific about what type to use. Frequently, egg whites replace whole eggs to reduce fat and cholesterol. All include generous amounts of natural flavorings—such as vanilla extract, spices, citrus zest, molasses, and brown sugar—to provide a full measure of flavor without unnecessary fat.

In this chapter you'll find meringue cookies, drop cookies, and cookies that you shape or slice and bake. See the recipes on pages 104 through 109 for several yummy bar cookies.

From top: *Peppermint Meringue Sticks and Chocolate Meringues*

CHOCOLATE MERINGUES

1 (16-ounce) carton vanilla low-fat yogurt
2 teaspoons unsweetened cocoa
3 egg whites
¼ teaspoon cream of tartar
⅛ teaspoon salt
¼ cup sugar
¾ cup sifted powdered sugar
½ teaspoon ground cinnamon
1 (1-ounce) square semisweet chocolate, grated
1 tablespoon finely chopped toasted almonds

Place a colander in a medium bowl; line with four layers of cheesecloth, allowing cheesecloth to extend over outside edges. Spoon yogurt into lined colander. Cover with plastic wrap; chill 12 hours.

Spoon yogurt cheese into a bowl; discard liquid. Stir in cocoa; cover and chill 12 hours.

Cover 2 cookie sheets with parchment paper. Draw 23 (3- x 1-inch) rectangles, 1 inch apart, on paper. Turn paper over; secure to cooking sheet with masking tape, and set aside.

Beat egg whites, cream of tartar, and salt at high speed of an electric mixer until foamy. Gradually add ¼ cup sugar, 1 tablespoon at a time, beating until soft peaks form. Combine powdered sugar and cinnamon; gradually add to egg white mixture, 1 tablespoon at a time, beating until stiff peaks form. (Do not underbeat.) Gently fold in chocolate.

Spoon egg white mixture into a pastry bag fitted with a No. 8 round tip; pipe in a zigzag motion down center of an outlined rectangle. Starting at one corner of rectangle, pipe meringue in a spiral fashion to trace rectangle. (Spiral sides should touch zigzag line down center, forming a solid base and ¼-inch-high sides for each bar.) Repeat procedure.

Bake at 200° for 2½ hours or until dry. Turn oven off, and cool meringues in closed oven at least 12 hours. Carefully remove meringues from paper.

Spoon yogurt mixture into a pastry bag fitted with a small star tip; pipe into centers of meringues. Sprinkle almonds over filling. Serve immediately. Yield: 23 bars.

PER BAR: 51 CALORIES (16% FROM FAT)
FAT 0.9G (SATURATED FAT 0.4G)
PROTEIN 1.6G CARBOHYDRATE 9.8G
CHOLESTEROL 1MG SODIUM 32MG

PEPPERMINT MERINGUE STICKS

Turn to page 90 to learn more about the techniques of beating egg whites for meringue.

3 egg whites
¼ teaspoon cream of tartar
⅛ teaspoon salt
¼ cup sugar
¾ cup sifted powdered sugar
¾ teaspoon peppermint extract
Red food coloring
1½ (1-ounce) squares semisweet chocolate

Cover a cookie sheet with parchment paper. Draw 56 (4-inch) lines 1 inch apart on paper. Turn paper over; secure to cookie sheet with masking tape, and set aside.

Beat first 3 ingredients at high speed of an electric mixer until foamy. Gradually add ¼ cup sugar, 1 tablespoon at a time, beating until soft peaks form. Gradually add powdered sugar, 1 tablespoon at a time, beating until stiff peaks form. (Do not underbeat.) Fold in peppermint extract.

Fit a large pastry bag with a No. 6 round tip. Using a cotton swab, heavily "paint" 6 straight lines lengthwise up inside of bag with red food coloring. Spoon mixture into bag, and pipe onto lines on parchment.

Bake at 200° for 1 hour or until dry. Turn oven off, and cool meringues in closed oven at least 12 hours. Carefully remove meringues from paper, and arrange in a single layer on plates.

Place chocolate in a heavy-duty, zip-top plastic bag; seal bag. Submerge bag in boiling water until chocolate melts. Snip a tiny hole in one corner of bag; drizzle chocolate over baked meringues. Freeze 10 minutes so that chocolate hardens. Store in an airtight container. Yield: 56 cookies.

PER COOKIE: 14 CALORIES (13% FROM FAT)
FAT 0.2G (SATURATED FAT 0.2G)
PROTEIN 0.2G CARBOHYDRATE 3.0G
CHOLESTEROL 0MG SODIUM 8MG

WHITE CHOCOLATE CHIP COOKIES

⅔ cup sugar
⅔ cup firmly packed brown sugar
¼ cup plus 3 tablespoons stick margarine, softened
¼ cup skim milk
1 teaspoon vanilla extract
¼ teaspoon butter flavoring
2 eggs
3½ cups all-purpose flour
1½ teaspoons baking soda
½ teaspoon salt
⅔ cup vanilla-flavored milk chips
Vegetable cooking spray

Combine first 7 ingredients in a large bowl; beat at medium speed of an electric mixer until blended. Combine flour, soda, and salt; add to margarine mixture, beating well. Add chips; stir well.

Drop dough by rounded tablespoonfuls, 2 inches apart, onto cookie sheets coated with cooking spray. Bake at 350° for 12 minutes. Remove from cookie sheets; cool on wire racks. Yield: 4½ dozen.

PER COOKIE: 82 CALORIES (29% FROM FAT)
FAT 2.6G (SATURATED FAT 1.1G)
PROTEIN 1.2G   CARBOHYDRATE 13.1G
CHOLESTEROL 8MG   SODIUM 82MG

FYI

To bake cookies all the same size, spoon cookie dough in equal amounts onto cookie sheets. Allow at least 2 inches between cookies.

OATMEAL-RAISIN HERMITS

Make sure the raisins you use are fresh and soft. Dry raisins will absorb the moisture from the cookie dough, making the cookies dry.

1½ cups all-purpose flour
¾ teaspoon baking powder
¾ teaspoon baking soda
¼ teaspoon salt
½ teaspoon ground cinnamon
⅛ teaspoon ground nutmeg
1¼ cups firmly packed brown sugar
¼ cup plus 2 tablespoons stick margarine, melted
2 tablespoons light-colored corn syrup
1 tablespoon vanilla extract
1 tablespoon water
3 egg whites
1⅔ cups regular oats, uncooked
1⅔ cups raisins
⅓ cup chopped pecans, toasted
Vegetable cooking spray

Combine first 6 ingredients; stir well. Combine brown sugar and next 5 ingredients in a large bowl; beat at medium speed of an electric mixer until well blended. Stir in oats, raisins, and pecans; let stand 5 minutes. Stir in flour mixture.

Drop dough by level tablespoonfuls, 2 inches apart, onto cookie sheets coated with cooking spray. Bake at 350° for 12 minutes or until almost set. Cool on cookie sheets 2 minutes or until firm. Remove from cookie sheets; cool on wire racks. Yield: 3½ dozen.

PER COOKIE: 97 CALORIES (24% FROM FAT)
FAT 2.6G (SATURATED FAT 0.4G)
PROTEIN 1.5G   CARBOHYDRATE 17.5G
CHOLESTEROL 0MG   SODIUM 71MG

ORANGE-BUTTERSCOTCH COOKIES

¼ cup plus 2 tablespoons stick margarine,
    softened
½ cup sugar
½ cup firmly packed brown sugar
¼ cup fat-free egg substitute
2 tablespoons skim milk
1 teaspoon grated orange rind
1 tablespoon unsweetened orange juice
1½ cups all-purpose flour
2 teaspoons baking powder
½ teaspoon salt
¼ teaspoon ground nutmeg
⅓ cup butterscotch morsels
Vegetable cooking spray

Beat margarine at medium speed of an electric
mixer until creamy; gradually add sugars, beating
well. Add egg substitute and next 3 ingredients;
beat well. Combine flour and next 3 ingredients;
add to margarine mixture, stirring just until blended.
Stir in butterscotch morsels.

Drop dough by level tablespoonfuls, 2 inches apart,
onto cookie sheets coated with cooking spray. Bake
at 375° for 7 to 8 minutes or until edges are golden.
Cool on cookie sheets 1 minute. Remove from cookie
sheets; cool on wire racks. Yield: 40 cookies.

PER COOKIE: 63 CALORIES (31% FROM FAT)
FAT 2.2G (SATURATED FAT 0.6G)
PROTEIN 0.7G CARBOHYDRATE 10.0G
CHOLESTEROL 0MG SODIUM 74MG

ALMOND SUGAR COOKIES

3 tablespoons sugar
⅛ teaspoon ground cinnamon
1 cup sugar
¼ cup plus 3 tablespoons stick margarine,
    softened
¼ cup skim milk
½ teaspoon almond extract
½ teaspoon vanilla extract
1 egg white
2½ cups all-purpose flour
¼ cup ground almonds
⅛ teaspoon salt
Vegetable cooking spray

Combine 3 tablespoons sugar and cinnamon in a
bowl; stir well. Set aside.

Beat 1 cup sugar and margarine at medium speed
of an electric mixer until light and fluffy. Add milk
and next 3 ingredients; beat well. Combine flour,
almonds, and salt; add to butter mixture, beating well.

Divide dough in half; cover and chill 1 portion.
Shape remaining dough into 30 (1-inch) balls; roll
balls in sugar mixture, coating well. Place balls,
2 inches apart, on cookie sheets coated with cooking spray. Flatten each ball with bottom of a glass.
Bake at 325° for 14 minutes. Remove from cookie
sheets; cool on wire racks. Repeat procedure with
remaining dough. Yield: 5 dozen.

PER COOKIE: 50 CALORIES (31% FROM FAT)
FAT 1.7G (SATURATED FAT 0.3G)
PROTEIN 0.8G CARBOHYDRATE 8.1G
CHOLESTEROL 0MG SODIUM 22MG

Steps to Success

Making light cookies is a lot like conducting
a science experiment—the right balance of ingredients is crucial. Here are some tips.

• If the batter seems dry and you're tempted to
add more liquid, don't. If you do, the cookie may
be cakelike and spread too much.

• Use stick margarine instead of tub margarine.
Unless indicated, do not use low-fat margarine or
anything that's labeled "spread."

• Preheat the oven unless otherwise indicated.

• Coat the cookie sheet with cooking spray
only if directed.

• If your cookie sheets have a nonstick coating,
watch the cookies carefully as they bake; dark-
surfaced pans of this type tend to make cookies
brown more quickly.

From left: *Peasecods (recipe on page 102) and Almond Cakes*

ALMOND CAKES

Find rose water in the spice section of large supermarkets.

1 cup blanched almonds
1⅓ cups sugar
1 cup all-purpose flour
1 teaspoon rose water (optional)
3 egg whites
Vegetable cooking spray

Position knife blade in food processor bowl; add almonds, and process until finely ground. Add sugar and flour; process until blended. Add rose water, if desired; add egg whites. Process until well blended (mixture will be very thick).

Shape dough into 28 balls, using floured hands; place balls, 2 inches apart, on cookie sheets coated with cooking spray. Bake at 325° for 28 minutes or until crisp on outside and soft on inside. Remove from cookie sheets; cool on wire racks. Yield: 28 cookies.

PER COOKIE: 88 CALORIES (32% FROM FAT)
FAT 3.1G (SATURATED FAT 0.3G)
PROTEIN 2.2G   CARBOHYDRATE 13.5G
CHOLESTEROL 0MG   SODIUM 6MG

CINNAMON SUGAR COOKIES

The cookie dough will be slightly sticky, so it helps to flour your hands before shaping the dough into balls.

1½ tablespoons sugar
⅛ teaspoon ground cinnamon
3 tablespoons reduced-calorie stick margarine, softened
⅔ cup sugar
1 egg
1½ teaspoons vanilla extract
1½ cups all-purpose flour
½ teaspoon baking soda
½ teaspoon ground cinnamon
1½ teaspoons all-purpose flour

Combine 1½ tablespoons sugar and ⅛ teaspoon cinnamon in a small bowl; set aside.

Beat margarine at medium speed of an electric mixer until creamy; gradually add ⅔ cup sugar, beating well. Add egg and vanilla; beat well. Combine 1½ cups flour, baking soda, and ½ teaspoon cinnamon; gradually add to margarine mixture, beating well.

Sprinkle 1½ teaspoons flour evenly over work surface. Turn dough out onto floured surface. Lightly flour hands, and shape dough into 26 balls. Roll balls in cinnamon-sugar mixture. Place balls, 3 inches apart, on ungreased cookie sheets. Pat each into a 2-inch circle. Bake at 375° for 6 to 8 minutes or until golden. Remove from cookie sheets; cool completely on wire racks. Yield: 26 cookies.

PER COOKIE: 60 CALORIES (17% FROM FAT)
FAT 1.1G (SATURATED FAT 0.1G)
PROTEIN 1.0G CARBOHYDRATE 11.4G
CHOLESTEROL 8MG SODIUM 40MG

LEMON SNAPS

2 cups all-purpose flour
2 teaspoons baking powder
¼ teaspoon baking soda
1 cup sugar
1 tablespoon grated lemon rind, divided
½ teaspoon ground ginger
¼ cup plus 2½ tablespoons stick margarine, softened
2 teaspoons light-colored corn syrup
2 teaspoons vanilla extract
1 egg
3 tablespoons sugar
Vegetable cooking spray

Combine first 3 ingredients in a bowl; stir well, and set aside.

Position knife blade in food processor bowl; add 1 cup sugar, 2 teaspoons lemon rind, and ginger. Process 1 minute or until lemon-colored, scraping sides of bowl once.

Spoon sugar mixture into a large bowl; add margarine. Beat at medium speed of an electric mixer until light and fluffy. Add corn syrup, vanilla, and egg; beat well. Stir in flour mixture (dough will be stiff).

Combine remaining 1 teaspoon lemon rind and 3 tablespoons sugar in a small bowl; stir well.

Coat hands lightly with cooking spray, and shape dough into 60 (1-inch) balls. Roll balls in lemon-sugar mixture. Place balls, 2 inches apart, on cookie sheets coated with cooking spray. Flatten balls with bottom of a glass. Bake at 375° for 7 minutes; cool on cookie sheets 5 minutes. Remove cookies from cookie sheets; cool on wire racks. Yield: 5 dozen.

PER COOKIE: 44 CALORIES (29% FROM FAT)
FAT 1.4G (SATURATED FAT 0.3G)
PROTEIN 0.6G CARBOHYDRATE 7.4G
CHOLESTEROL 4MG SODIUM 34MG

RASPBERRY THUMBPRINTS

1½ cups all-purpose flour
½ teaspoon baking powder
¼ teaspoon baking soda
¼ teaspoon salt
¼ cup cornstarch
¼ cup plus 3 tablespoons stick margarine,
    softened
½ cup sugar
2 tablespoons light-colored corn syrup
2½ teaspoons vanilla extract
½ teaspoon grated lemon rind
⅛ teaspoon almond extract
1 egg
Vegetable cooking spray
¼ cup seedless raspberry jam

Combine first 5 ingredients; stir well. Combine margarine and next 6 ingredients in a large bowl; beat at medium speed of an electric mixer until well blended. Stir in flour mixture; cover and freeze 30 minutes or until firm.

Shape dough into 36 (1-inch) balls. Place balls, 1 inch apart, on cookie sheets coated with cooking spray. Press thumb into center of each cookie, leaving an indentation. Spoon about ¼ teaspoon jam into center of each cookie.

Bake at 375° for 10 minutes; cool 2 minutes or until firm. Remove from cookie sheets, and cool on wire racks. Yield: 3 dozen.

PER COOKIE: 65 CALORIES (33% FROM FAT)
FAT 2.4G (SATURATED FAT 0.5G)
PROTEIN 0.8G CARBOHYDRATE 10.0G
CHOLESTEROL 6MG SODIUM 61MG

APRICOT PINWHEELS

1 cup apricot preserves
¾ cup minced dried apricots
2½ tablespoons unsweetened orange juice
2¾ cups all-purpose flour
¾ teaspoon baking powder
¼ teaspoon baking soda
¼ teaspoon salt
¼ cup stick margarine, softened
1 cup sugar
½ cup firmly packed brown sugar
2½ tablespoons vegetable oil
½ teaspoon vanilla extract
3 egg whites
Vegetable cooking spray

Combine first 3 ingredients in a small saucepan; bring to a boil. Reduce heat to medium-low, and cook 10 minutes, stirring occasionally. Remove from heat; cover and cool completely.

Combine flour and next 3 ingredients; stir well, and set aside. Place margarine in a large mixing bowl; beat at medium speed of an electric mixer until light and fluffy. Gradually add sugars, beating at medium speed until well blended. Add oil, vanilla, and egg whites; beat well. Add flour mixture; beat until well blended.

Divide dough in half. Working with 1 portion at a time (cover remaining dough to keep from drying out), gently press dough into a 4-inch square on heavy-duty plastic wrap; cover with additional plastic wrap. Roll each half of dough, still covered, into a 12-inch square. Chill 30 minutes.

Remove top sheet of plastic wrap; spoon apricot mixture evenly over dough squares. Roll up each square, jellyroll fashion, peeling plastic wrap from bottom of dough while rolling. (Dough may be soft.) Wrap each roll individually in plastic wrap, and freeze 8 hours.

Cut each roll into 24 (½-inch) slices; place slices, 1 inch apart, on cookie sheets coated with cooking spray. Bake at 350° for 10 minutes. Remove from cookie sheets; cool on wire racks. Yield: 4 dozen.

PER COOKIE: 89 CALORIES (18% FROM FAT)
FAT 1.8G (SATURATED FAT 0.3G)
PROTEIN 1.1G CARBOHYDRATE 17.7G
CHOLESTEROL 0MG SODIUM 45MG

From top: *Raspberry Thumbprints and Apricot Pinwheels*

PEASECODS

(pictured on page 98)

*These sweet treats, when properly made,
resemble pea pods. The Pilgrims referred
to any legume or pod as a peasecod.*

2 cups all-purpose flour
¼ cup sugar
½ teaspoon ground cinnamon
¼ cup chilled stick margarine, cut into small
     pieces
½ cup skim milk
1 egg yolk, lightly beaten
1 cup whole pitted dates
1 cup raisins
2 tablespoons sugar
2 tablespoons stick margarine
½ teaspoon ground ginger
½ teaspoon ground cinnamon
1 egg white
½ teaspoon water
Vegetable cooking spray
1 tablespoon sugar, divided

Combine first 3 ingredients in a large bowl; cut
in ¼ cup chilled margarine with a pastry blender.
Combine milk and egg yolk; add to flour mixture,
stirring until a dough forms. Turn dough out onto a
floured surface; knead 3 or 4 times. Wrap in heavy-
duty plastic wrap, and chill 1 hour.

Position knife blade in food processor bowl; add
dates and next 5 ingredients. Process until smooth.
Set aside. Combine egg white and water; beat with
a wire whisk, and set aside. Divide dough in half;
cover and chill 1 portion of dough. Turn remaining
portion out onto a lightly floured surface, and roll to
⅛-inch thickness; cut into 18 rounds, using a 3-inch
cutter. Working with 1 round at a time, gently
grasp opposite edges, and pull into an oval shape.
Moisten edges of dough with egg white mixture.

Spoon 1 teaspoon date mixture onto half of each
oval. Fold dough over filling; seal edges by pressing
with a fork dipped in flour. Carefully place on
cookie sheets coated with cooking spray; brush tops
with egg white mixture, and sprinkle with 1½ teaspoons sugar. Repeat procedure with remaining

dough, date mixture, egg white mixture, and
remaining 1½ teaspoons sugar. Bake at 375° for 15
minutes or until lightly browned. Remove from
cookie sheets; cool on wire racks. Yield: 3 dozen.

PER COOKIE: 79 CALORIES (25% FROM FAT)
FAT 2.2G (SATURATED FAT 0.5G)
PROTEIN 1.2G   CARBOHYDRATE 14.4G
CHOLESTEROL 6MG   SODIUM 26MG

TOASTED ALMOND
BISCOTTI

*See page 10 for the proper way to measure flour
and other ingredients.*

2 cups all-purpose flour
¾ teaspoon baking soda
¼ teaspoon salt
1 cup sugar
½ cup slivered almonds, chopped and toasted
2 eggs, lightly beaten
1 egg white, lightly beaten
½ teaspoon vanilla extract
¼ teaspoon almond extract
Vegetable cooking spray

Combine first 5 ingredients in a large bowl. Combine eggs and next 3 ingredients; add to flour mixture, stirring until well blended (dough will be dry).

Turn dough out onto a lightly floured surface;
knead 7 or 8 times. Shape dough into a 16-inch-
long roll. Place roll on a cookie sheet coated with
cooking spray, and flatten to 1-inch thickness.

Bake at 350° for 30 minutes. Remove roll from
cookie sheet to a wire rack; cool 10 minutes. Cut
diagonally into 30 (½-inch) slices; place slices, cut
sides down, on cookie sheets. Reduce oven temperature to 325°; bake 10 minutes. Turn cookies over;
bake 10 minutes. (Cookies will be slightly soft in
center but will harden as they cool.) Remove from
cookie sheets; cool on wire racks. Yield: 2½ dozen.

PER COOKIE: 72 CALORIES (16% FROM FAT)
FAT 1.3G (SATURATED FAT 0.2G)
PROTEIN 1.7G   CARBOHYDRATE 13.5G
CHOLESTEROL 15MG   SODIUM 26MG

From left: *Toasted Almond Biscotti and Gingered White Chocolate Biscotti*

GINGERED WHITE CHOCOLATE BISCOTTI

2 cups all-purpose flour
1 teaspoon baking soda
½ teaspoon salt
⅔ cup sugar
2 tablespoons minced crystallized
    ginger
1 (4-ounce) bar premium white chocolate,
    finely chopped (about ¾ cup)
2 eggs, lightly beaten
1 egg white, lightly beaten
1 teaspoon vanilla extract
Vegetable cooking spray

Combine first 6 ingredients in a large bowl. Combine eggs, egg white, and vanilla; add to flour mixture, stirring until well blended (dough will be dry).

Turn dough out onto a lightly floured surface; knead 7 or 8 times. Shape dough into a 16-inch-long roll.

Place roll on a cookie sheet coated with cooking spray, and flatten roll to 1-inch thickness.

Bake at 350° for 30 minutes. Remove roll from cookie sheet to a wire rack; cool 10 minutes.

Cut roll diagonally into 24 (½-inch) slices; place slices, cut sides down, on cookie sheets. Reduce oven temperature to 325°; bake 10 minutes. Turn cookies over, and bake 10 additional minutes. (Cookies will be slightly soft in center but will harden as they cool.) Remove from cookie sheets, and cool completely on wire racks. Yield: 2 dozen.

PER COOKIE: 96 CALORIES (20% FROM FAT)
FAT 2.1G (SATURATED FAT 1.1G)
PROTEIN 2.0G   CARBOHYDRATE 17.3G
CHOLESTEROL 19MG   SODIUM 114MG

CHOCOLATE-MINT BISCOTTI

1¾ cups all-purpose flour
¾ teaspoon baking soda
¼ teaspoon salt
1 cup sugar
⅓ cup unsweetened cocoa
⅓ cup mint chocolate morsels, chopped
3 tablespoons slivered almonds, chopped and toasted
2 eggs
1 egg white
2 tablespoons crème de menthe
1 tablespoon all-purpose flour
Vegetable cooking spray

Combine first 7 ingredients in a bowl. Combine eggs, egg white, and crème de menthe, stirring well with a wire whisk. Slowly add egg mixture to flour mixture, stirring just until dry ingredients are moistened. (Mixture will be very stiff.)

Sprinkle 1 tablespoon flour evenly over work surface. Turn dough out onto floured surface; knead 7 or 8 times. Divide dough in half; shape each portion into an 8-inch log. Place logs, 4 inches apart, on a cookie sheet coated with cooking spray. Bake at 325° for 40 minutes; remove from oven, and cool 15 minutes.

Carefully cut each log diagonally into 15 (½-inch) slices; place, cut sides down, on cookie sheets. Reduce oven temperature to 300°, and bake 18 additional minutes. (Cookies will be slightly soft in center but will harden as they cool.) Remove from cookie sheets, and cool completely on wire racks. Yield: 2½ dozen.

PER COOKIE: 80 CALORIES (16% FROM FAT)
FAT 1.4G (SATURATED FAT 0.5G)
PROTEIN 1.8G CARBOHYDRATE 14.6G
CHOLESTEROL 15MG SODIUM 58MG

EASY CHOCOLATE-CARAMEL BROWNIES

Use a cake mix that contains pudding, such as Pillsbury. The recipe won't work otherwise. Also, a shiny metal baking pan is recommended.

2 tablespoons skim milk
27 small soft caramel candies (about 8 ounces)
½ cup fat-free sweetened condensed milk (not evaporated skim milk)
1 (18.25-ounce) package devil's food cake mix with pudding
¼ cup plus 3 tablespoons reduced-calorie stick margarine, melted
1 egg white, lightly beaten
Vegetable cooking spray
1 teaspoon all-purpose flour
½ cup reduced-fat chocolate baking chips

Combine skim milk and candies in a microwave-safe bowl. Microwave at HIGH 1½ to 2 minutes or until caramels melt and mixture is smooth, stirring with a wire whisk after every minute. Set aside.

Combine sweetened condensed milk and next 3 ingredients; stir well (batter will be very stiff). Coat bottom only of a 13- x 9- x 2-inch baking pan with cooking spray; dust lightly with flour. Press two-thirds of batter into prepared pan, using floured hands; pat evenly (layer will be thin).

Bake at 350° for 10 minutes. Remove from oven; sprinkle with chocolate chips. Drizzle caramel mixture over chips; carefully drop remaining batter by spoonfuls over caramel mixture. Bake at 350° for 30 minutes. Cool completely in pan on a wire rack. Cut into bars. Yield: 3 dozen.

Note: If you use a baking pan with a dark surface, reduce the oven temperature to 325°.

PER BROWNIE: 122 CALORIES (30% FROM FAT)
FAT 4.0G (SATURATED FAT 1.6G)
PROTEIN 1.6G CARBOHYDRATE 20.4G
CHOLESTEROL 1MG SODIUM 224MG

Easy Chocolate-Caramel Brownies

COFFEE BROWNIES

1½ cups firmly packed dark brown sugar
½ cup reduced-calorie stick margarine
2½ tablespoons instant coffee granules
1 tablespoon vanilla extract
2 egg whites
1 egg
2 cups all-purpose flour
2 teaspoons baking powder
⅛ teaspoon salt
½ cup semisweet chocolate morsels
Vegetable cooking spray

Combine first 3 ingredients in a small saucepan. Cook over medium heat 4 minutes or until margarine melts and mixture is smooth, stirring often.
Combine sugar mixture, vanilla, egg whites, and egg; beat at low speed of an electric mixer until smooth. Combine flour, baking powder, and salt; add to creamed mixture, beating well. Stir in chocolate morsels. Spread batter in a 13- x 9- x 2-inch baking pan coated with cooking spray. Bake at 350° for 18 minutes; cool. Cut into bars. Yield: 2 dozen.

PER BROWNIE: 129 CALORIES (24% FROM FAT)
FAT 3.5G (SATURATED FAT 1.1G)
PROTEIN 1.8G   CARBOHYDRATE 23.0G
CHOLESTEROL 9MG   SODIUM 105MG

FUDGY MINT BROWNIES

¼ cup stick margarine, softened
¾ cup sugar
2 tablespoons water
2 teaspoons vanilla extract
1 egg
¾ cup all-purpose flour
¼ teaspoon baking powder
⅛ teaspoon salt
⅓ cup unsweetened cocoa
8 hard round peppermint candy pieces, crushed
1 egg white
Vegetable cooking spray

Beat margarine at medium speed of an electric mixer until creamy; add sugar, beating well. Add water, vanilla, and egg; beat well. Combine flour and next 4 ingredients; add to margarine mixture, stirring just until moistened. Beat egg white at high speed until stiff peaks form; gently fold into cocoa mixture.
Pour batter into an 8-inch square pan coated with cooking spray. Bake at 350° for 25 minutes. Cool in pan on a wire rack. Cut into bars. Yield: 1 dozen.

PER BROWNIE: 144 CALORIES (30% FROM FAT)
FAT 4.8G (SATURATED FAT 1.1G)
PROTEIN 2.4G   CARBOHYDRATE 23.0G
CHOLESTEROL 19MG   SODIUM 95MG

APPLE-SPICE BARS

1 cup all-purpose flour
½ cup whole wheat flour
1 teaspoon baking soda
¼ teaspoon salt
1 teaspoon ground cinnamon
¼ teaspoon ground cloves
¼ cup reduced-calorie stick margarine, softened
½ cup firmly packed brown sugar
1 cup unsweetened applesauce
1 teaspoon vanilla extract
1 cup finely chopped unpeeled cooking apple
1 cup currants
½ cup regular oats, uncooked
⅓ cup butterscotch morsels
Vegetable cooking spray

Combine first 6 ingredients; stir well. Beat margarine at medium speed of an electric mixer; add sugar, beating at medium speed until light and fluffy. Add flour mixture to margarine mixture alternately with applesauce, beginning and ending with flour mixture. Stir in vanilla. Stir in apple and next 3 ingredients. Pour batter into an 11- x 7- x 2-inch baking dish coated with cooking spray.
Bake at 350° for 40 minutes or until a wooden pick inserted in center comes out clean. Cool in pan on a wire rack. Cut into bars. Yield: 2 dozen.

PER BAR: 92 CALORIES (19% FROM FAT)
FAT 1.9G (SATURATED FAT 0.5G)
PROTEIN 1.4G   CARBOHYDRATE 18.2G
CHOLESTEROL 0MG   SODIUM 101MG

LEMON SOUFFLÉ BARS

¼ cup stick margarine, softened
⅓ cup sugar
1 egg white
½ teaspoon vanilla extract
1¼ cups all-purpose flour
⅛ teaspoon salt
Vegetable cooking spray
1 (8-ounce) carton fat-free egg substitute
1 cup sugar
½ cup all-purpose flour
½ teaspoon baking powder
1 tablespoon freshly grated lemon rind
⅓ cup lemon juice
2 teaspoons powdered sugar

Beat margarine at medium speed of an electric mixer until creamy; add ⅓ cup sugar, beating well. Add egg white and vanilla, beating mixture well.

Combine 1¼ cups flour and salt; add to margarine mixture, stirring well. Pat into bottom of a 13- x 9- x 2-inch baking dish coated with cooking spray. Bake at 375° for 15 minutes or until lightly browned.

Combine egg substitute and 1 cup sugar; beat at medium speed until blended.

Combine ½ cup flour and baking powder. Add flour mixture, lemon rind, and lemon juice to egg substitute mixture; stir well. Pour mixture over baked crust. Bake at 350° for 18 to 20 minutes or until set. Cool completely on a wire rack. Sprinkle with powdered sugar. Cool in pan on a wire rack. Cut into bars. Yield: 3 dozen.

PER BAR: 67 CALORIES (17% FROM FAT)
FAT 1.3G (SATURATED FAT 0.3G)
PROTEIN 1.4G   CARBOHYDRATE 12.6G
CHOLESTEROL 0MG   SODIUM 40MG

Lemon Soufflé Bars

Raspberry-Oatmeal Squares

RASPBERRY-OATMEAL SQUARES

1 (10-ounce) package frozen raspberries in
  light syrup, thawed
2 tablespoons sugar
2 tablespoons cornstarch
¼ teaspoon almond extract
⅓ cup stick margarine, softened
⅔ cup firmly packed brown sugar
1 teaspoon vanilla extract
1 cup quick-cooking oats, uncooked
¾ cup all-purpose flour
¼ cup whole wheat flour
½ teaspoon baking soda
⅛ teaspoon salt
Vegetable cooking spray

  Combine first 3 ingredients in a saucepan; stir until smooth. Bring to a boil, stirring constantly; cook, stirring constantly, 1 minute or until thickened. Remove from heat; stir in almond extract, and set aside.

  Beat margarine at medium speed of an electric mixer until fluffy; add brown sugar, beating well. Add vanilla; beat well.

  Combine oats and next 4 ingredients in a medium bowl; stir well. Add to margarine mixture, stirring until mixture resembles coarse meal.

  Press 2 cups oats mixture evenly into bottom of a 9-inch square baking pan coated with cooking spray; set remaining oats mixture aside. Bake at 375° for 6 to 8 minutes or until crust looks puffed.

  Spread raspberry mixture over prepared crust; top with remaining oats mixture, gently pressing into raspberry mixture. Bake at 375° for 15 to 17 minutes or until golden. Cool completely in pan on a wire rack. Cut into squares. Yield: 16 squares.

PER SQUARE: 144 CALORIES (26% FROM FAT)
FAT 4.2G (SATURATED FAT 0.8G)
PROTEIN 1.8G   CARBOHYDRATE 25.3G
CHOLESTEROL 0MG   SODIUM 92MG

STRAWBERRY-OAT SQUARES

(pictured on page 92)

Enjoy these cool and creamy squares as a light dessert or snack.

¾ cup sifted cake flour
½ cup quick-cooking oats, uncooked
⅓ cup sifted powdered sugar
⅓ cup chilled stick margarine, cut into small pieces
Vegetable cooking spray
½ (4-ounce) block ⅓-less-fat cream cheese
½ (4-ounce) block nonfat cream cheese
½ cup nonfat cottage cheese
¼ cup sugar
¼ teaspoon lemon extract
1 (10-ounce) package frozen strawberry halves in syrup, thawed and undrained
½ cup canned crushed pineapple in juice, undrained
1 tablespoon cornstarch
Strawberry slices (optional)
Mint sprigs (optional)

Combine first 3 ingredients in a medium bowl; cut in margarine with a pastry blender until mixture resembles coarse meal. Press oats mixture into bottom of an 8-inch square pan coated with cooking spray. Bake at 350° for 10 to 12 minutes or until lightly browned.

Position knife blade in food processor bowl; add cheeses, sugar, and lemon extract. Process until smooth. Spoon over prepared crust. Set aside.

Combine thawed strawberries (with syrup), pineapple (with juice), and cornstarch in a small saucepan; stir until smooth. Cook over medium heat, stirring constantly, until thickened. Spoon over cheese mixture. Bake at 350° for 12 minutes; cool completely. Cover and chill thoroughly. Cut into squares. If desired, garnish each square with a strawberry slice and a mint sprig. Yield: 16 squares.

PER SQUARE: 122 CALORIES (36% FROM FAT)
FAT 4.9G (SATURATED FAT 1.3G)
PROTEIN 2.9G CARBOHYDRATE 17.1G
CHOLESTEROL 4MG SODIUM 109MG

PEANUT BUTTER-OAT SQUARES

Cut the baked mixture into squares while it's warm. Once it cools, it tends to crumble when cut.

2 cups regular oats, uncooked
1 cup crisp rice cereal
⅓ cup firmly packed brown sugar
¼ cup light-colored corn syrup
2 tablespoons reduced-calorie stick margarine
¼ cup reduced-fat peanut butter spread
½ teaspoon vanilla extract
Vegetable cooking spray

Combine oats and rice cereal in a large bowl, stirring well; set aside.

Combine brown sugar, corn syrup, and margarine in a small saucepan. Cook over medium-high heat, stirring constantly, until margarine melts. Remove from heat; add peanut butter spread and vanilla, stirring until well blended. Pour peanut butter mixture over cereal mixture; stir well.

Press cereal mixture firmly into an 8-inch square pan coated with cooking spray. Bake at 250° for 45 minutes or until golden. Cool in pan 10 minutes; cut into squares. Cool squares completely in pan. Yield: 16 squares.

PER SQUARE: 87 CALORIES (29% FROM FAT)
FAT 2.8G (SATURATED FAT 0.4G)
PROTEIN 1.9G CARBOHYDRATE 14.4G
CHOLESTEROL 0MG SODIUM 46MG

FYI

Be sure to bake bar cookies in the size pan indicated; otherwise the baking time and texture of the cookie may be affected. Use a shiny metal pan if the recipe calls for a baking pan, and glass if the recipe recommends a baking dish.

Streusel Apple Pie (recipe on page 113)

PIES, TARTS & PASTRIES

Wouldn't it be great if you could indulge in rich-tasting pies and pastries yet stay true to your low-fat resolutions? You can when you follow the recipes and suggestions on the next several pages. Start with the recipe for Streusel Apple Pie (page 113). Like several of the recipes in this chapter, it combines a basic pastry crust with a luscious, low-fat filling to keep calories from fat under 30 percent.

With the recipes that begin on page 117, you can even enjoy old-fashioned fruit cobblers—comfort food at its best. Peach-Almond Cobbler (page 121) is as delicious as its traditional counterpart and will please cobbler lovers everywhere.

Turn to pages 122 through 125 to try a fruit-filled tart or turnover. Both turnovers use phyllo dough to create especially flaky crusts. If you've never used phyllo, don't worry—the photos on page 124 will show you how easy it is to work with.

Steps to Pastry Success

Here's how to make flaky pastries.

• Cut fat into the flour, using a pastry blender or two knives, until mixture resembles coarse meal.

• After sprinkling with water or buttermilk, stir just enough to moisten dry ingredients. Add the minimum liquid needed to moisten the flour mixture; don't overwork the dough.

• Chill the dough to make it easier to handle and to help keep the crust from becoming soggy.

• Use an ovenproof glass pieplate or dull metal piepan. Shiny metal pans reflect heat and prevent the crust from browning.

• If the pastry will be baked before you add the filling, prick the crust generously with a fork before baking; this will prevent it from becoming puffy. Do not prick the pastry if the pie filling will be added to the unbaked crust.

Cut margarine into flour mixture with a pastry blender until mixture resembles coarse meal.

After tossing with the liquid, gently press mixture into a 4-inch circle on heavy-duty plastic wrap; cover with more plastic wrap.

Roll dough, still covered, into an 11-inch circle, about ⅛ inch thick.

Pinch edge of pastry with your fingers to flute; repeat about every ¼ inch.

Basic Pastry

1 cup all-purpose flour
1 teaspoon sugar
¼ teaspoon salt
¼ cup chilled stick margarine, cut into pieces
3 tablespoons nonfat buttermilk
Vegetable cooking spray

Combine first 3 ingredients in a bowl; cut in margarine with a pastry blender until mixture resembles coarse meal and is pale yellow (about 3½ minutes). Sprinkle buttermilk over mixture; toss with a fork until dry ingredients are moistened and mixture is crumbly.

Gently press mixture into a 4-inch circle on heavy-duty plastic wrap; cover with additional plastic wrap, and chill 15 minutes. Roll dough, still covered, into an 11-inch circle. Remove plastic wrap, and fit dough into a 9-inch pieplate coated with cooking spray. Roll edge under, and flute edge of pastry as desired. Yield: 8 servings.

PER SERVING: 112 CALORIES (47% FROM FAT)
FAT 5.9G (SATURATED FAT 1.2G)
PROTEIN 1.9G CARBOHYDRATE 12.8G
CHOLESTEROL 0MG SODIUM 146MG

Food Processor Pastry

1 cup all-purpose flour
1 teaspoon sugar
¼ teaspoon salt
3 tablespoons shortening
3½ tablespoons ice water
Vegetable cooking spray

Position knife blade in food processor bowl; add first 3 ingredients, and pulse 2 or 3 times. Add shortening, and pulse 6 times or until mixture resembles coarse meal. With processor running, slowly add ice water through food chute, processing just until combined (do not form a ball).

Press mixture gently into a 4-inch circle on heavy-duty plastic wrap; cover with additional plastic wrap. Roll dough, still covered, into an 11-inch circle; chill 10 minutes or until plastic wrap can be removed easily. Remove bottom sheet of plastic wrap; fit dough into a 9-inch pieplate coated with cooking spray, and remove top sheet of plastic wrap. Flute edge of pastry as desired. Yield: 8 servings.

PER SERVING: 94 CALORIES (39% FROM FAT)
FAT 4.1G (SATURATED FAT 0.9G)
PROTEIN 1.6G CARBOHYDRATE 12.4G
CHOLESTEROL 0MG SODIUM 74MG

Streusel Apple Pie

(pictured on page 110)

Food Processor Pastry (at left)
1 (4-inch) piece vanilla bean, split
   lengthwise
¼ cup firmly packed brown sugar
1½ tablespoons all-purpose flour
½ teaspoon ground cinnamon
2½ pounds Rome or other cooking apples,
   peeled, cored, and thinly sliced
¼ cup all-purpose flour
½ cup firmly packed brown sugar
¼ cup regular oats, uncooked
¼ teaspoon ground cinnamon
3 tablespoons chilled stick margarine, cut into
   small pieces

Prepare Food Processor Pastry; set aside.

Scrape seeds from vanilla bean into a large bowl; discard bean. Add ¼ cup brown sugar, 1½ table-spoons flour, and ½ teaspoon cinnamon to vanilla seeds; stir well. Add apple slices; toss well to coat. Spoon mixture into prepared pastry shell. Cover with aluminum foil, and bake at 350° for 45 minutes or until apple mixture is crisp-tender.

Combine ¼ cup flour and next 3 ingredients; cut in margarine until mixture is crumbly. Uncover pie, and sprinkle with oats mixture. Bake, uncovered, 25 additional minutes. Yield: 8 servings.

Note: Substitute 1 teaspoon vanilla extract for vanilla bean, if desired.

PER SERVING: 308 CALORIES (27% FROM FAT)
FAT 9.1G (SATURATED FAT 1.8G)
PROTEIN 2.8G CARBOHYDRATE 56.2G
CHOLESTEROL 0MG SODIUM 132MG

BLUEBERRY CRUMBLE PIE

*Don't worry when the pie doesn't hold its shape. The blueberries are
supposed to spill out—that's the crumble.*

5 cups fresh or frozen blueberries, thawed
1 (9-inch) reduced-fat graham cracker
    crust
¾ cup firmly packed brown sugar
3 tablespoons all-purpose flour
1½ teaspoons vanilla extract
¼ teaspoon grated lemon rind
1 (8-ounce) carton low-fat sour cream
¼ cup fine, dry breadcrumbs
1 tablespoon sugar
1 tablespoon stick margarine, melted

Place blueberries in crust. Combine brown sugar
and next 4 ingredients; spread over blueberries.
Combine breadcrumbs, 1 tablespoon sugar, and
margarine; sprinkle over sour cream mixture. Bake
at 375° for 40 minutes or until filling is set and
crumbs are lightly browned. Cool on a wire rack
1 hour. Yield: 8 servings.

PER SERVING: 312 CALORIES (24% FROM FAT)
FAT 8.4G (SATURATED FAT 2.5G)
PROTEIN 3.2G   CARBOHYDRATE 56.5G
CHOLESTEROL 11MG   SODIUM 166MG

Blueberry Crumble Pie

OVEN-FRIED PEACH PIES

1 cup drained canned peaches in light syrup, chopped
3 tablespoons sugar, divided
¾ teaspoon ground cinnamon, divided
1 tablespoon all-purpose flour
1 (10-ounce) can refrigerated buttermilk biscuits
Butter-flavored vegetable cooking spray

Combine peaches, 2 tablespoons sugar, and ½ teaspoon cinnamon.

Sprinkle flour over work surface. Separate biscuits; place on floured surface. Roll each biscuit into a 4½-inch circle. Place 1 heaping tablespoon peach mixture over half of each circle. Brush edges of circles with water; fold in half. Seal edges by pressing with a fork.

Place pies on an ungreased cookie sheet; coat pies with cooking spray. Combine remaining 1 tablespoon sugar and ¼ teaspoon cinnamon; sprinkle mixture over pies. Bake at 375° for 10 minutes. Yield: 10 pies.

PER PIE: 107 CALORIES (22% FROM FAT)
FAT 2.6G (SATURATED FAT 1.0G)
PROTEIN 2.2G CARBOHYDRATE 19.9G
CHOLESTEROL 0MG SODIUM 281MG

SPICED PUMPKIN PIE

Food Processor Pastry (page 113)
1½ cups canned pumpkin
⅓ cup sugar
¾ cup evaporated skimmed milk
½ cup fat-free egg substitute
¼ cup reduced-calorie maple syrup
½ teaspoon ground cinnamon
¼ teaspoon ground cloves
¼ teaspoon ground allspice
2 cups vanilla nonfat frozen yogurt

Prepare Food Processor Pastry; set aside.

Combine pumpkin and next 7 ingredients in a large bowl; stir well. Pour mixture into pastry shell. Bake at 350° for 1 hour or until a knife inserted in center comes out clean. Cool completely on a wire rack. To serve, cut into 8 slices, and top each slice with ¼ cup frozen yogurt. Yield: 8 servings.

PER SERVING: 209 CALORIES (19% FROM FAT)
FAT 4.4G (SATURATED FAT 1.0G)
PROTEIN 7.0G CARBOHYDRATE 36.3G
CHOLESTEROL 1MG SODIUM 158MG

PUMPKIN-PRALINE PIE

Food Processor Pastry (page 113)
1¾ cups canned pumpkin
1 cup 2% low-fat milk
½ cup firmly packed brown sugar
1 tablespoon all-purpose flour
3 tablespoons maple syrup
2 tablespoons bourbon
½ teaspoon salt
1½ teaspoons ground cinnamon
1½ teaspoons vanilla extract
¼ teaspoon ground ginger
¼ teaspoon ground nutmeg
¼ teaspoon ground allspice
2 egg whites, lightly beaten
1 egg, lightly beaten
⅓ cup coarsely chopped pecans
¼ cup firmly packed brown sugar
1½ teaspoons dark corn syrup
½ teaspoon vanilla extract

Prepare Food Processor Pastry. Prick bottom and sides of pastry generously with a fork. Bake at 400° for 15 minutes; cool on a wire rack.

Combine pumpkin and next 13 ingredients; stir well with a wire whisk. Pour into prepared crust; bake at 400° for 40 minutes.

Combine pecans, ¼ cup brown sugar, corn syrup, and ½ teaspoon vanilla; stir well. Sprinkle pecan mixture over pie, and bake 15 additional minutes or until filling is set (shield edges of piecrust with aluminum foil, if necessary). Cool completely on a wire rack. Yield: 8 servings.

PER SERVING: 292 CALORIES (28% FROM FAT)
FAT 9.0G (SATURATED FAT 2.1G)
PROTEIN 5.4G CARBOHYDRATE 46.3G
CHOLESTEROL 30MG SODIUM 270MG

RAISIN CIDER PIE

Basic Pastry (page 113)
4 cups peeled, coarsely chopped Granny Smith
    apple (about 3 large)
1 cup raisins
½ cup sugar
1½ cups unsweetened apple cider
½ teaspoon grated lemon rind
1 tablespoon lemon juice
½ teaspoon ground cinnamon
¼ teaspoon salt
2 tablespoons cornstarch
2 tablespoons water

Prepare Basic Pastry; set aside.

Combine apple and next 7 ingredients in a saucepan; bring to a boil. Combine cornstarch and 2 tablespoons water, stirring well. Add cornstarch mixture to apple mixture, stirring constantly.

Cook, stirring constantly, until mixture thickens and begins to boil. Pour hot mixture into prepared pastry shell. Bake at 400° for 10 minutes. Reduce heat to 350° (do not remove pie from oven); bake 40 to 45 minutes or until filling is hot and bubbly. Cool completely on a wire rack. Yield: 8 servings.

PER SERVING: 277 CALORIES (20% FROM FAT)
FAT 6.2G (SATURATED FAT 1.2G)
PROTEIN 2.6G   CARBOHYDRATE 55.3G
CHOLESTEROL 0MG   SODIUM 223MG

STRAWBERRY-RHUBARB PIE

Basic Pastry (page 113)
1 cup sugar
3 tablespoons cornstarch
½ teaspoon grated orange rind
⅓ cup unsweetened orange juice
2½ cups sliced fresh rhubarb
1½ cups halved fresh strawberries
3 tablespoons all-purpose flour
3 tablespoons brown sugar
2 tablespoons quick-cooking oats, uncooked
½ teaspoon ground cinnamon
2 tablespoons chilled reduced-calorie stick
    margarine, cut into small pieces

Prepare Basic Pastry; set aside. Combine 1 cup sugar and cornstarch in a saucepan; stir. Stir in orange rind and juice. Bring to a boil; cook, stirring constantly, 1 minute. Remove from heat. Add rhubarb and strawberries; stir gently. Spoon into pastry shell.

Combine 3 tablespoons flour and next 3 ingredients in a bowl; cut in margarine with a pastry blender until mixture resembles coarse meal. Sprinkle over rhubarb mixture. Bake at 400° for 30 minutes. Cool completely on a wire rack. Yield: 8 servings.

PER SERVING: 280 CALORIES (26% FROM FAT)
FAT 8.0G (SATURATED FAT 1.4G)
PROTEIN 2.8G   CARBOHYDRATE 50.7G
CHOLESTEROL 0MG   SODIUM 177MG

Pies and the Freezer

Some baked pies—especially fruit and pumpkin pies—freeze well, although some changes in texture should be expected. The pastry may lose some crispness during freezing and defrosting, and fruit will soften slightly.

To freeze a baked pie, place it in the freezer unwrapped. After the pie freezes, wrap it securely. Then label, date, and place back in the freezer; serve it within two months. Thaw the baked pie at room temperature 30 minutes; bake at 350° until warm, if desired.

You can also freeze uncooked pastry up to two months. Shape the pastry into a ball, or roll it into a circle to freeze flat or in the pieplate. Either way, wrap the pastry securely, label, and date.

Summer Blackberry Cobbler

SUMMER BLACKBERRY COBBLER

8 cups fresh blackberries, divided
1 cup sugar
⅓ cup cornstarch
2 tablespoons reduced-calorie stick margarine
½ teaspoon ground cinnamon
½ teaspoon almond extract
Vegetable cooking spray
Food Processor Pastry (page 113)
2 teaspoons skim milk
1 tablespoon sugar

Combine 6 cups blackberries and next 5 ingredients in a saucepan. Bring to a boil over medium heat, stirring occasionally; cook 1 minute or until thickened. Remove from heat; cool slightly.

Gently stir remaining 2 cups blackberries into saucepan. Pour mixture into an 8-inch square baking dish coated with cooking spray. Cool mixture completely.

Prepare dough for Food Processor Pastry; place dough between two sheets of heavy-duty plastic wrap; gently press into a 4-inch square. Chill 20 minutes. Roll into an 8-inch square. Place in freezer 5 minutes or until wrap can be removed easily. Remove top sheet of plastic wrap. Cut pastry into ½-inch strips. Arrange strips lattice-style over blackberry mixture; seal strips to edge of dish. Brush strips with milk; sprinkle with 1 tablespoon sugar. Bake at 375° for 45 to 50 minutes or until pastry is golden and filling is bubbly. Yield: 8 servings.

PER SERVING: 309 CALORIES (19% FROM FAT)
FAT 6.6G (SATURATED FAT 1.2G)
PROTEIN 2.7G   CARBOHYDRATE 62.3G
CHOLESTEROL 0MG   SODIUM 103MG

Tart Cherry Cobbler

TART CHERRY COBBLER

7 cups pitted, halved tart cherries
1 cup sugar
¼ cup cornstarch
1 teaspoon ground cinnamon
½ teaspoon almond extract
Vegetable cooking spray
1 cup all-purpose flour
½ teaspoon baking powder
½ teaspoon baking soda
¼ teaspoon salt
¼ cup sugar
1 cup low-fat sour cream
2 tablespoons skim milk
1 teaspoon vanilla extract
1 egg
1 tablespoon sugar

Combine first 4 ingredients in a large saucepan; stir well. Bring to a boil over medium heat; cook 1 minute or until thickened. Remove from heat; stir in almond extract. Spoon into an 11- x 7- x 2-inch baking dish coated with cooking spray; set aside.

Position knife blade in food processor bowl; add flour and next 4 ingredients. Pulse 2 times or until blended. Add sour cream and next 3 ingredients; process until well blended. Spread batter over cherry mixture. Sprinkle with 1 tablespoon sugar. Bake at 350° for 30 minutes or until filling is bubbly and topping is golden. Serve warm. Yield: 10 servings.

PER SERVING: 254 CALORIES (14% FROM FAT)
FAT 3.9G (SATURATED FAT 2.0G)
PROTEIN 3.7G   CARBOHYDRATE 52.7G
CHOLESTEROL 30MG   SODIUM 141MG

CINNAMON-APPLE SKILLET COBBLER

¼ cup plus 3 tablespoons sugar, divided
1 tablespoon stick margarine
6 Granny Smith apples (about 2¾ pounds),
    peeled, cored, and cut into 8 wedges each
2 tablespoons cornstarch
1 teaspoon ground cinnamon
2 teaspoons grated lemon rind, divided
¾ cup all-purpose flour
½ teaspoon baking powder
3 tablespoons stick margarine, melted
2 teaspoons vinegar

Combine ¼ cup sugar and 1 tablespoon margarine in a 10-inch cast-iron skillet; cook over medium heat 5 minutes or until mixture is golden, stirring often.

Combine apple wedges, cornstarch, cinnamon, and 1 teaspoon lemon rind; toss gently. Layer apple mixture in skillet; sprinkle with 2 tablespoons sugar.

Combine flour, baking powder, remaining 1 tablespoon sugar, and remaining 1 teaspoon lemon rind in a bowl, stirring well. Combine melted margarine and vinegar; add to flour mixture. Stir with a fork just until dry ingredients are moistened. Shape into a ball.

Place dough between two sheets of heavy-duty plastic wrap. Roll dough to a 10½-inch circle. Remove top sheet of plastic wrap; invert over apple mixture. Remove remaining sheet of plastic wrap. Cut slits in pastry to allow steam to escape. Bake at 375° for 45 minutes or until apple wedges are tender and crust is golden. Yield: 8 servings.

PER SERVING: 211 CALORIES (26% FROM FAT)
FAT 6.2G (SATURATED FAT 1.1G)
PROTEIN 1.4G CARBOHYDRATE 39.5G
CHOLESTEROL 0MG SODIUM 86MG

DRIED-FRUIT COBBLER WITH MOLASSES BISCUITS

1½ cups water
1 cup unsweetened orange juice
⅓ cup orange marmalade
2 (8-ounce) bags mixed dried fruit, coarsely
    chopped
1 cup all-purpose flour
1 teaspoon baking powder
⅛ teaspoon baking soda
¼ teaspoon ground cinnamon
Dash of ground cloves
⅓ cup chilled stick margarine, cut into small
    pieces
2 tablespoons skim milk
2 tablespoons molasses
1 tablespoon orange marmalade
2 teaspoons water

Combine first 4 ingredients in a 2-quart baking dish; stir well. Bake at 400° for 30 minutes.

Combine flour and next 4 ingredients; cut in margarine with a pastry blender until mixture resembles coarse meal. Combine milk and molasses; add to flour mixture, stirring just until dry ingredients are moistened.

Turn dough out onto a lightly floured surface, and knead 5 or 6 times. Roll dough to ½-inch thickness; cut into 10 biscuits with a 2-inch biscuit cutter. Remove fruit mixture from oven; arrange biscuits over hot fruit mixture. Bake 20 additional minutes or until biscuits are golden.

Combine 1 tablespoon marmalade and 2 teaspoons water; brush over biscuits. Serve warm. Yield: 10 servings.

PER SERVING: 276 CALORIES (20% FROM FAT)
FAT 6.2G (SATURATED FAT 1.2G)
PROTEIN 2.4G CARBOHYDRATE 55.6G
CHOLESTEROL 0MG SODIUM 146MG

Peach-Almond Cobbler

PEACH-ALMOND COBBLER

If fresh peaches are out of season, substitute the same amount of frozen peach slices. Just thaw them before you use them.

2 cups all-purpose flour
1 tablespoon sugar
¼ teaspoon salt
¼ cup plus 2 tablespoons chilled stick margarine, cut into 6 pieces
¼ cup plus 2 tablespoons ice water
Vegetable cooking spray
6 cups peeled, sliced peaches (about 3¾ pounds)
¾ cup firmly packed brown sugar, divided
2½ tablespoons all-purpose flour
1 tablespoon vanilla extract
1 teaspoon ground cinnamon
¼ cup slivered almonds
1 egg, lightly beaten
1 teaspoon water
1 tablespoon sugar

Position knife blade in food processor bowl; add first 3 ingredients. Pulse 2 or 3 times. Add margarine pieces, and pulse 10 times or until mixture resembles coarse meal. With processor running, slowly add ice water through food chute, processing just until combined (do not form a ball).

Gently press flour mixture into a 4-inch circle on heavy-duty plastic wrap; cover with additional plastic wrap. Roll dough, still covered, into a 15- x 13-inch rectangle. Place dough in freezer 5 minutes or until plastic wrap can be removed easily. Remove top sheet of plastic wrap. Invert dough, and fit it into a 2-quart baking dish coated with cooking spray, allowing dough to extend over edges of dish; remove top sheet of plastic wrap.

Combine peach slices, ½ cup brown sugar, 2½ tablespoons flour, vanilla, and cinnamon; toss gently. Spoon peach mixture into prepared crust; fold edges of dough over peach mixture (it will cover peaches only partially). Sprinkle remaining ¼ cup brown sugar over peach mixture; sprinkle with almonds.

Combine egg and 1 teaspoon water; stir well. Brush egg mixture over dough; sprinkle with 1 tablespoon sugar. Bake at 375° for 45 minutes or until filling is bubbly and crust is lightly browned. Let stand 30 minutes before serving. Yield: 10 servings.

PER SERVING: 302 CALORIES (27% FROM FAT)
FAT 9.2G (SATURATED FAT 1.6G)
PROTEIN 4.5G CARBOHYDRATE 51.5G
CHOLESTEROL 11MG SODIUM 149MG

PEAR COBBLER

6 cups peeled, sliced pear (about 3 pounds)
⅓ cup firmly packed brown sugar
1 tablespoon all-purpose flour
1 tablespoon lemon juice
½ teaspoon apple pie spice
Vegetable cooking spray
½ cup all-purpose flour
½ cup whole wheat flour or all-purpose flour
1 teaspoon baking powder
¼ teaspoon salt
3 tablespoons brown sugar
2 tablespoons chilled stick margarine, cut into small pieces
½ cup skim milk
2 teaspoons stick margarine, melted
1 tablespoon brown sugar

Combine first 5 ingredients in a large bowl; toss gently to coat. Spoon pear mixture into an 8-inch square baking dish coated with cooking spray.

Combine ½ cup all-purpose flour, whole wheat flour, and next 3 ingredients; cut in 2 tablespoons chilled margarine with a pastry blender until mixture resembles coarse meal. Add milk, and toss with a fork until dry ingredients are moistened.

Drop dough by heaping tablespoonfuls onto pear mixture. Brush melted margarine over dough, and sprinkle with 1 tablespoon brown sugar. Bake at 350° for 45 minutes or until bubbly and lightly browned. Yield: 8 servings.

PER SERVING: 232 CALORIES (18% FROM FAT)
FAT 4.6G (SATURATED FAT 0.8G)
PROTEIN 3.0G CARBOHYDRATE 47.7G
CHOLESTEROL 0MG SODIUM 183MG

APRICOT-APPLE STREUSEL TART

1 cup plus 2 tablespoons sifted cake flour
1 tablespoon sugar
½ teaspoon baking powder
2 tablespoons chilled stick margarine, cut into
    small pieces
¼ cup plain nonfat yogurt
¾ cup thinly sliced dried apricot halves
2 tablespoons raisins
¼ cup unsweetened orange juice
2 tablespoons amaretto
6 cups peeled, chopped Golden Delicious apple
½ cup firmly packed brown sugar
1 tablespoon plus 1 teaspoon cornstarch
⅛ teaspoon ground cardamom
⅛ teaspoon ground coriander
½ cup regular oats, uncooked
1 tablespoon all-purpose flour
1 tablespoon brown sugar
1 tablespoon chilled stick margarine
2 tablespoons sliced almonds

Combine first 3 ingredients; cut in 2 tablespoons margarine with a pastry blender until mixture resembles coarse meal and is pale yellow. Add yogurt, 1 tablespoon at a time, tossing with a fork until moistened and crumbly. (Do not form a ball.)

Gently press mixture into a 4-inch circle onto heavy-duty plastic wrap; cover with additional plastic wrap. Roll dough, still covered, into a 12½-inch circle. Place dough in freezer 30 minutes or until wrap can be removed easily. Remove bottom sheet of wrap. Fit dough into an 11-inch round tart pan; remove top sheet of wrap. Place in freezer.

Combine apricots and next 3 ingredients in a large bowl; let stand 30 minutes, stirring occasionally. Add apple and next 4 ingredients; stir well. Spoon mixture into pastry shell. Set aside.

Position knife blade in food processor bowl; add oats, and process until finely ground. Add flour, 1 tablespoon brown sugar, and 1 tablespoon margarine; process 5 seconds or until combined. Stir in almonds; sprinkle over apple mixture. Cover with aluminum foil, and bake at 400° for 30 minutes. Uncover and reduce heat to 375° (do not remove

tart from oven). Bake 30 minutes or until lightly browned. Cool on a wire rack. Yield: 12 servings.

PER SERVING: 198 CALORIES (18% FROM FAT)
FAT 3.9G (SATURATED FAT 0.7G)
PROTEIN 2.4G   CARBOHYDRATE 39.0G
CHOLESTEROL 0MG   SODIUM 59MG

LA TARTE TATIN

1 cup sifted cake flour
½ cup plus 3 tablespoons sugar, divided
3 tablespoons chilled stick margarine, cut into
    small pieces
2 tablespoons ice water
5 medium-size Golden Delicious apples (about 2
    pounds), each peeled and cut into 8 wedges
1 tablespoon lemon juice
2 tablespoons brown sugar
¼ cup plus 2 tablespoons vanilla low-fat yogurt
1 tablespoon low-fat sour cream

Combine flour and 2 tablespoons sugar; cut in margarine with a pastry blender until mixture resembles coarse meal. Sprinkle ice water, 1 tablespoon at a time, over surface; toss until moistened and crumbly. (Do not form a ball.) Press into a 4-inch circle on heavy-duty plastic wrap. Cover with plastic wrap; chill 15 minutes. Roll dough, still covered, into an 11-inch circle. Place in freezer 10 minutes.

Combine apples, 1 tablespoon sugar, and lemon juice; toss. Let stand 15 minutes. Wrap handle of a 10-inch heavy skillet with aluminum foil. Sprinkle remaining ½ cup sugar in skillet; place over medium heat. Caramelize by stirring often until sugar melts and is golden. Add apple mixture; cook 5 minutes, stirring constantly. Remove from heat.

Remove plastic wrap from dough. Place dough over apples in skillet, tucking dough around edge of skillet. Cut slits in dough. Bake at 425° for 20 minutes or until browned. Invert onto a platter.

Combine brown sugar, yogurt, and sour cream; stir well. Drizzle over warm tart. Yield: 8 servings.

PER SERVING: 229 CALORIES (20% FROM FAT)
FAT 5.0G (SATURATED FAT 1.1G)
PROTEIN 1.9G   CARBOHYDRATE 46.1G
CHOLESTEROL 1MG   SODIUM 59MG

La Tarte Tatin

*Spoon pear mixture onto 1
end of each phyllo stack.*

*Fold left bottom corner over
pear mixture, forming a
triangle.*

*Keep folding back and forth
into triangle to end of the
phyllo strip.*

Pear Phyllo Pastries

Pear Phyllo Pastries

¼ cup fine, dry breadcrumbs
¼ cup firmly packed brown sugar
3 tablespoons stick margarine, melted
1 tablespoon vegetable oil
½ cup sugar
½ teaspoon ground cinnamon
½ teaspoon almond extract
¼ teaspoon ground nutmeg
4 cups peeled, coarsely chopped pear (about
    4 pears)
½ cup dried cranberries
¼ cup chopped almonds, toasted
12 sheets frozen phyllo dough, thawed
Vegetable cooking spray

Combine breadcrumbs and brown sugar in a
bowl; stir well, and set aside. Combine melted
margarine and oil; stir well, and set aside.

Combine ½ cup sugar and next 3 ingredients in a
large bowl; stir well. Add pear, cranberries, and
almonds; toss gently to coat.

Working with 1 phyllo sheet at a time (cover
remaining dough to keep from drying out), brush
1 sheet lightly with margarine mixture. Stack 1
phyllo sheet on top of first; brush top sheet lightly
with margarine mixture. Repeat procedure with a
third phyllo sheet, forming a stack of 3 sheets.
Sprinkle 2 tablespoons breadcrumb mixture over
stack. Using a sharp knife or pizza cutter, cut stack
lengthwise into 3 (4½-inch-wide) strips.

Spoon about ⅓ cup pear mixture onto 1 end of
each phyllo strip. Fold left bottom corner over pear
mixture, forming a triangle. Keep folding back and
forth into triangle to end of strip. Repeat procedure
with remaining sheets of phyllo, margarine mixture,
breadcrumb mixture, and pear mixture.

Place triangles, seam sides down, on a baking
sheet coated with cooking spray. Bake at 350° for
25 minutes or until golden. Serve warm or at room
temperature. Yield: 12 servings.

Note: If dried cranberries are unavailable, substitute dried currants or raisins.

PER SERVING: 216 CALORIES (28% FROM FAT)
FAT 6.6G (SATURATED FAT 1.1G)
PROTEIN 2.5G CARBOHYDRATE 38.4G
CHOLESTEROL 0MG SODIUM 150MG

Brandied Prune Turnovers

2 cups chopped pitted prunes (about ¾ pound)
½ cup water
¼ cup plus 2 tablespoons brandy
1 tablespoon water
1 teaspoon cornstarch
¼ cup plus 2 tablespoons brown sugar
¼ cup plus 2 tablespoons chopped almonds or
    pecans, toasted
12 sheets frozen phyllo dough, thawed
Butter-flavored vegetable cooking spray
1 tablespoon powdered sugar

Combine first 3 ingredients in a small saucepan;
bring to a boil. Reduce heat; simmer, uncovered, 5
minutes. Combine 1 tablespoon water and cornstarch; stir well. Add cornstarch mixture to prune
mixture; stir well. Stir in brown sugar. Bring to a
boil; cook, stirring constantly, 1 minute. Remove
from heat, and cool. Stir in almonds.

Working with 1 phyllo sheet at a time (cover
remaining dough to keep from drying out), heavily
coat 1 sheet with cooking spray. Stack 1 phyllo
sheet on top of first; coat top sheet with cooking
spray. Using a pizza cutter or scissors, cut stack
lengthwise into 4 (3½-inch-wide) strips. Spoon
about 1½ tablespoons prune mixture on 1 short
side of each phyllo strip; fold left bottom corner
over mixture, forming a triangle. Keep folding
back and forth into triangle to end of strip. Repeat
procedure with remaining sheets of phyllo and
prune mixture.

Place triangles, seam sides down, on a baking
sheet coated with cooking spray; lightly coat with
cooking spray. Bake at 350° for 20 minutes or until
golden. Cool completely on a wire rack. Sprinkle
with powdered sugar. Yield: 2 dozen.

PER TURNOVER: 98 CALORIES (19% FROM FAT)
FAT 2.1G (SATURATED FAT 0.3G)
PROTEIN 1.4G CARBOHYDRATE 16.6G
CHOLESTEROL 0MG SODIUM 54MG

Brownie Cheesecake Torte (recipe on page 129)

DESSERT POTPOURRI

*W*hoever first said that if it tastes good it must be bad for you never tasted Brownie Cheesecake Torte (page 129). It received rave reviews from the taste-testing panel—maybe even as much applause as Banana-Caramel Custard (page 136) and Fudge Soufflé Cake with Turtle Sauce (page 139).

This chapter offers a variety of baked dessert favorites including cheesecakes, custards, puddings, and soufflés as well as fruit crisps and crumbles. Reduced levels of calories and fat help each recipe achieve an excellent nutrient rating. And even the most discriminating food lover will applaud the winning taste.

Triple-Chocolate Cheesecake

TRIPLE-CHOCOLATE CHEESECAKE

This luscious cheesecake tastes like a creamy frozen fudge pop.

¼ cup sugar
1 tablespoon stick margarine, softened
1 tablespoon egg white
1⅓ cups chocolate graham cracker
    crumbs
Vegetable cooking spray
½ cup low-fat sour cream
1 tablespoon sugar
2 teaspoons unsweetened cocoa
3 tablespoons dark rum
3 (1-ounce) squares semisweet chocolate

¼ cup chocolate syrup
1 (8-ounce) block nonfat cream cheese,
    softened
1 (8-ounce) block ⅓-less-fat cream cheese,
    softened
1 cup sugar
2 tablespoons unsweetened cocoa
1 teaspoon vanilla extract
¼ teaspoon salt
2 eggs
Chocolate curls (optional)

Place first 3 ingredients in a mixing bowl; beat at medium speed of an electric mixer until blended. Add graham cracker crumbs; stir well. Firmly press mixture into bottom and 1 inch up sides of an 8-inch springform pan coated with cooking spray. Bake at 350° for 10 minutes; cool on a wire rack.

Combine sour cream, 1 tablespoon sugar, and 2 teaspoons cocoa; stir well, and set aside.

Combine rum and chocolate squares in top of a double boiler. Cook over simmering water 2 minutes or until chocolate melts, stirring often. Remove from heat; add chocolate syrup, stirring until smooth.

Place cheeses in a large bowl; beat at medium speed until smooth. Add 1 cup sugar and next 3 ingredients; beat until smooth. Add rum mixture; beat at low speed until well blended. Add eggs, one at a time, beating well after each addition.

Pour cheese mixture into prepared crust; bake at 300° for 40 minutes or until almost set. Turn oven off, and spread sour cream mixture over cheesecake. Let cheesecake stand in closed oven 45 minutes. Remove cheesecake from oven, and cool to room temperature. Cover and chill at least 8 hours. Garnish with chocolate curls, if desired. Yield: 12 servings.

PER SERVING: 260 CALORIES (35% FROM FAT)
FAT 10.1G (SATURATED FAT 5.5G)
PROTEIN 7.5G CARBOHYDRATE 35.9G
CHOLESTEROL 57MG SODIUM 205MG

Steps to Success

Here are a few hints to help you achieve the perfect cheesecake.

• Don't overbeat the cream cheese mixture. The more air you incorporate, the more likely the cheesecake is to crack.

• Abrupt changes in temperature also tend to make the cheesecake crack. Let it cool to room temperature before chilling.

• How to know when a cheesecake is done? It should be set around the edges, but wiggle slightly in the center when you shake the pan.

BROWNIE CHEESECAKE TORTE
(pictured on page 126)

1 (15.1-ounce) package low-fat fudge brownie mix
2 teaspoons instant coffee granules
½ teaspoon ground cinnamon
1 (4-ounce) jar carrot baby food
Vegetable cooking spray
½ cup plus 2 tablespoons sugar, divided
1 tablespoon plus 1 teaspoon all-purpose flour
1 teaspoon vanilla extract
1 (8-ounce) block ⅓-less-fat cream cheese, softened
1 (8-ounce) block nonfat cream cheese, softened
2 egg whites
3 tablespoons skim milk, divided
2 tablespoons unsweetened cocoa
Chocolate syrup (optional)
Fresh raspberries (optional)

Combine first 4 ingredients. Firmly press mixture into bottom and 1 inch up sides of a 9-inch springform pan coated with cooking spray. Set aside.

Combine ½ cup sugar and next 4 ingredients; beat at medium speed of an electric mixer until well blended. Add egg whites and 2 tablespoons milk; beat well. Combine ½ cup batter, remaining 1 tablespoon milk, remaining 2 tablespoons sugar, and cocoa; stir well. Spoon remaining batter alternately with cocoa mixture into prepared crust. Swirl together, using tip of a knife.

Bake at 425° for 10 minutes. Reduce oven temperature to 250° (do not remove pan from oven). Bake 45 minutes or until set. Cool completely on a wire rack. Garnish with chocolate syrup and fresh raspberries, if desired. Yield: 12 servings.

Note: This recipe was tested with SnackWell's fudge brownie mix.

PER SERVING: 277 CALORIES (24% FROM FAT)
FAT 7.5G (SATURATED FAT 3.8G)
PROTEIN 7.9G CARBOHYDRATE 44.1G
CHOLESTEROL 18MG SODIUM 338MG

LEMON CHEESECAKE

1 (32-ounce) carton vanilla low-fat yogurt
Vegetable cooking spray
1 cup low-fat granola cereal (without raisins)
1 tablespoon stick margarine, melted
1 cup nonfat sour cream
¾ cup sugar
3 tablespoons cornstarch
¼ teaspoon salt
1 (8-ounce) block ⅓-less-fat cream cheese,
    softened
1 teaspoon grated lemon rind
2 tablespoons fresh lemon juice
1½ teaspoons vanilla extract
2 eggs
2 egg whites
¾ cup low-fat sour cream
1 tablespoon sugar
1 teaspoon vanilla extract
1 egg white, lightly beaten
1 (10-ounce) package frozen raspberries in
    light syrup, thawed

Place a colander in a 2-quart bowl. Line with four layers of cheesecloth, allowing cheesecloth to extend over edge. Spoon yogurt into colander. Cover with plastic wrap; chill 12 hours. Spoon yogurt cheese into a bowl; discard liquid. Cover and chill.

Coat bottom of a 9-inch springform pan with cooking spray. Combine granola and margarine. Press into bottom of pan. Bake at 325° for 20 minutes; cool on a wire rack.

Add nonfat sour cream and next 4 ingredients to yogurt cheese; beat at medium speed of an electric mixer until smooth. Add lemon rind and next 4 ingredients; beat well. Spoon cheese mixture into crust. Bake at 325° for 1 hour; remove from oven.

Combine low-fat sour cream and next 3 ingredients; stir well. Spread over cheesecake; return to oven, and bake 15 minutes. Turn off oven; let cheesecake stand in closed oven 1 hour. Remove from oven; cover and chill at least 8 hours. Serve with raspberries. Yield: 12 servings.

PER SERVING: 244 CALORIES (34% FROM FAT)
FAT 9.2G (SATURATED FAT 4.7G)
PROTEIN 7.8G CARBOHYDRATE 32.6G
CHOLESTEROL 56MG SODIUM 202MG

CARAMEL SWIRL-APPLE CHEESECAKE

*Start this cheesecake a day ahead so the
yogurt will have ample time to drain
and become yogurt cheese.*

1 (32-ounce) carton vanilla low-fat yogurt
¼ cup sugar
1 tablespoon stick margarine, softened
1 egg white
1¼ cups graham cracker crumbs
1 teaspoon ground cinnamon
Vegetable cooking spray
¼ cup firmly packed brown sugar
¼ cup unsweetened orange juice
3 cups peeled, cubed Golden Delicious
    apple (about 1¼ pounds)
½ cup sugar
3 tablespoons cornstarch
1 tablespoon vanilla extract
¼ teaspoon salt
1 (8-ounce) block ⅓-less-fat cream cheese,
    softened
1 (8-ounce) block nonfat cream cheese,
    softened
2 eggs
⅓ cup plus 2 tablespoons fat-free
    caramel-flavored sundae syrup,
    divided
Cinnamon sticks (optional)

Place a colander in a 2-quart glass measure or bowl. Line colander with four layers of cheesecloth, allowing cheesecloth to extend over edge of bowl. Spoon yogurt into colander. Cover loosely with plastic wrap, and chill 12 hours. Spoon yogurt cheese into a bowl, discarding liquid. Cover yogurt cheese, and chill.

Combine ¼ cup sugar, margarine, and egg white in a mixing bowl; beat at medium speed of an electric mixer until blended. Add graham cracker crumbs and ground cinnamon; stir well. Firmly press mixture into bottom and 1½ inches up sides of a 9-inch springform pan coated with cooking spray. Bake at 350° for 10 minutes; cool on a wire rack.

Caramel Swirl-Apple Cheesecake

Combine brown sugar and orange juice in a large nonstick skillet; bring mixture to a boil. Add cubed apple; cook 8 minutes until apple is tender and liquid evaporates, stirring occasionally. Set apple mixture aside.

Combine yogurt cheese, ½ cup sugar, and next 5 ingredients in a mixing bowl; beat at medium speed of an electric mixer until mixture is smooth. Add eggs, one at a time, beating well after each addition.

Spoon apple mixture into prepared crust. Pour cheese mixture over apple mixture; top with ⅓ cup syrup, and swirl with a knife to create a marbled effect. Bake at 300° for 1 hour until cheesecake is almost set. Turn oven off; loosen cake from sides of pan, using a narrow metal spatula or knife. Let cheesecake stand in closed oven 40 minutes.

Remove cheesecake from oven, and cool to room temperature. Cover and chill at least 8 hours. Drizzle remaining 2 tablespoons syrup over cheese-cake; garnish with cinnamon sticks, if desired. Yield: 12 servings.

PER SERVING: 286 CALORIES (25% FROM FAT)
FAT 8.0G (SATURATED FAT 3.7G)
PROTEIN 10.4G   CARBOHYDRATE 44.2G
CHOLESTEROL 55MG   SODIUM 384MG

Blueberry-Cherry Crisp

BLUEBERRY-CHERRY CRISP

¼ cup low-fat sour cream
1 tablespoon plus 1 teaspoon light brown sugar
2 cups fresh blueberries
2 cups pitted fresh sweet cherries
½ cup all-purpose flour
2 tablespoons sugar
2 tablespoons light brown sugar
2 tablespoons stick margarine, melted

Combine sour cream and 1 tablespoon plus 1 teaspoon brown sugar in a bowl; stir well. Cover and chill at least 30 minutes.

Combine blueberries and cherries in an 8-inch square pan; toss well.

Combine flour and remaining 3 ingredients in a medium bowl; beat at medium speed of an electric mixer until mixture is crumbly. Sprinkle over blueberry mixture. Bake at 375° for 40 minutes or until lightly browned. To serve, spoon ½ cup fruit crisp into each individual serving bowl; top each serving with 2 teaspoons sour cream mixture. Yield: 4 servings.

PER SERVING: 276 CALORIES (28% FROM FAT)
FAT 8.6G (SATURATED FAT 2.4G)
PROTEIN 3.5G CARBOHYDRATE 49.1G
CHOLESTEROL 6MG SODIUM 81MG

SUNSHINE CRISP

½ cup flaked sweetened coconut
2 tablespoons sugar
1 tablespoon all-purpose flour
¼ teaspoon vanilla extract
Dash of salt
1 egg white
Vegetable cooking spray
2 tablespoons graham cracker crumbs
2 tablespoons stick margarine, melted
1 (15¼-ounce) can unsweetened crushed pineapple, undrained
¼ cup thinly sliced dried apricot halves
1 cup peeled, chopped mango
2 tablespoons sugar
2 tablespoons cornstarch
2 tablespoons water

Combine first 6 ingredients; stir well. Spread coconut mixture evenly on a baking sheet coated with cooking spray. Bake at 325° for 20 minutes or until edges are lightly browned. Cool completely.

Break coconut mixture into small pieces. Position knife blade in food processor bowl; add coconut pieces and cracker crumbs. Process until blended. With processor running, pour margarine through food chute, and process until blended. Set aside.

Drain pineapple, reserving ½ cup juice. Combine ¼ cup pineapple juice and apricot slices in a 1-cup glass measuring cup. Cover with heavy-duty plastic wrap, and vent. Microwave at HIGH 2½ minutes. Let stand, covered, 15 minutes; drain.

Combine apricots, remaining ¼ cup pineapple juice, pineapple, mango, and remaining 3 ingredients; stir well. Spoon fruit mixture into a 1-quart baking dish; sprinkle with coconut mixture. Bake at 350° for 35 minutes or until golden. Yield: 6 (½-cup) servings.

PER SERVING: 211 CALORIES (31% FROM FAT)
FAT 7.3G (SATURATED FAT 3.4G)
PROTEIN 1.8G CARBOHYDRATE 37.0G
CHOLESTEROL 0MG SODIUM 98MG

APPLE-OATMEAL CRUMBLE

7 large Granny Smith apples (about 3⅛ pounds), peeled, cored, and cut into ½-inch-thick wedges
½ cup firmly packed brown sugar
1 tablespoon cornstarch
2 tablespoons lemon juice
1 teaspoon ground cinnamon
1 teaspoon vanilla extract
½ teaspoon ground nutmeg
½ teaspoon ground allspice
½ cup plus 2 tablespoons regular oats, uncooked
¼ cup reduced-calorie stick margarine, cut into pieces
¼ cup firmly packed brown sugar
2 tablespoons all-purpose flour
Vegetable cooking spray

Combine first 8 ingredients in a large bowl; toss well. Let stand 20 minutes, stirring occasionally.

Position knife blade in food processor bowl; add oats. Pulse 3 or 4 times. Add margarine, ¼ cup brown sugar, and flour; pulse 3 or 4 times or until mixture resembles coarse meal.

Place apple mixture in a 13- x 9- x 2-inch baking dish coated with cooking spray; sprinkle oats mixture evenly over apple mixture. Cover and bake at 400° for 35 minutes; uncover and bake 20 additional minutes or until apple is tender and topping is lightly browned. Serve warm. Yield: 10 servings.

PER SERVING: 178 CALORIES (19% FROM FAT)
FAT 3.7G (SATURATED FAT 0.5G)
PROTEIN 1.1G CARBOHYDRATE 37.6G
CHOLESTEROL 0MG SODIUM 49MG

CRANBERRY-CHOCOLATE CRUMBLE

¾ cup water
½ cup sugar
1 (12-ounce) bag fresh or frozen cranberries, thawed
⅓ cup seedless raspberry jam
Vegetable cooking spray
2 tablespoons milk chocolate chips
½ cup all-purpose flour
⅓ cup regular oats, uncooked
¼ cup firmly packed brown sugar
3 tablespoons stick margarine, melted

Combine first 3 ingredients in a medium saucepan; bring to a boil. Reduce heat, and simmer 10 minutes, stirring occasionally. Remove from heat; stir in jam. Spoon mixture evenly into six 6-ounce custard cups coated with cooking spray; sprinkle with chocolate chips.

Combine flour and remaining 3 ingredients; toss well. Sprinkle evenly over cranberry mixture. Place cups on a baking sheet; bake at 350° for 20 minutes or until bubbly. Yield: 6 servings.

PER SERVING: 305 CALORIES (22% FROM FAT)
FAT 7.6G (SATURATED FAT 2.0G)
PROTEIN 2.5G CARBOHYDRATE 58.6G
CHOLESTEROL 2MG SODIUM 82MG

Cranberry-Chocolate Crumble

Gingered Pear and Plum Brown Betty

¼ cup unsweetened apple juice
2 tablespoons sugar
2 tablespoons all-purpose flour
2 tablespoons lemon juice
5 cups peeled, thinly sliced pear (about 2 pounds)
2½ cups thinly sliced plum (about ¾ pound)
Vegetable cooking spray
¾ cup gingersnap crumbs, divided (about 12 cookies)
½ cup quick-cooking oats, uncooked
⅓ cup firmly packed brown sugar
2 tablespoons all-purpose flour
3 tablespoons stick margarine, melted

Combine first 4 ingredients in a large bowl, and stir well. Add fruit, and toss well.

Place half of fruit mixture in an 11- x 7- x 2-inch baking dish coated with cooking spray; sprinkle with ½ cup gingersnap crumbs. Add remaining fruit mixture to dish.

Combine remaining ¼ cup gingersnap crumbs, oats, brown sugar, and 2 tablespoons flour; stir well. Add margarine, and toss well. Sprinkle crumb mixture over fruit mixture. Bake at 350° for 45 minutes or until fruit is tender. Yield: 8 servings.

PER SERVING: 279 CALORIES (25% FROM FAT)
FAT 7.9G (SATURATED FAT 1.6G)
PROTEIN 2.9G CARBOHYDRATE 52.2G
CHOLESTEROL 6MG SODIUM 74MG

Nectarine Pandowdy

6 cups peeled, sliced nectarine
⅔ cup sugar
⅛ teaspoon ground cinnamon
Vegetable cooking spray
1 (4-ounce) can refrigerated crescent dinner rolls
1 tablespoon sugar
Sugared Pecans

Combine first 3 ingredients in a bowl; toss well. Spoon mixture into a 9-inch pieplate coated with cooking spray. Bake at 350° for 15 minutes.

Unroll crescent roll dough, and separate along perforations into triangles; cut each triangle in half. Remove nectarine mixture from oven; arrange dough over hot nectarine mixture (dough will not cover entire surface). Coat dough with cooking spray; sprinkle with 1 tablespoon sugar. Bake at 350° for 20 minutes or until lightly browned.

Remove from oven; press crust into nectarine mixture with a spoon, allowing juices to moisten top of crust. Sprinkle Sugared Pecans over crust; bake 5 minutes. Serve warm. Yield: 6 servings.

Sugared Pecans
1 tablespoon sugar
1 tablespoon stick margarine
¼ cup chopped pecans
1 tablespoon unsweetened orange juice
¼ teaspoon ground cinnamon
Dash of ground red pepper
Vegetable cooking spray

Melt sugar and margarine in a small skillet over low heat. Remove from heat; stir in pecans and next 3 ingredients. Spread pecan mixture evenly on a baking sheet coated with cooking spray. Bake at 350° for 10 minutes, stirring after 5 minutes. Immediately scrape pecan mixture onto a sheet of aluminum foil coated with cooking spray, spreading pecan mixture evenly; cool completely. Break mixture into small pieces. Yield: ½ cup.

PER SERVING: 290 CALORIES (30% FROM FAT)
FAT 9.8G (SATURATED FAT 1.5G)
PROTEIN 2.9G CARBOHYDRATE 51.4G
CHOLESTEROL 0MG SODIUM 166MG

Nectarine Pandowdy

BANANA-CARAMEL CUSTARD

1 cup sugar
½ cup water
Vegetable cooking spray
2 cups 2% low-fat milk
4 eggs, lightly beaten
½ cup mashed ripe banana
¼ cup plus 2 tablespoons sugar
1 tablespoon vanilla extract
Mint sprigs (optional)

Combine 1 cup sugar and water in a small heavy saucepan over medium-high heat; cook until sugar dissolves. Continue cooking 12 additional minutes or until golden. Immediately pour into six 6-ounce ramekins or custard cups coated with cooking spray, tipping quickly until sugar coats bottoms of ramekins; set aside.

Heat milk over medium-high heat in a heavy saucepan to 180° or until tiny bubbles form around edge of pan (do not boil). Remove from heat.

Combine eggs and next 3 ingredients in a medium bowl; stir well. Gradually add hot milk, stirring with a wire whisk until blended.

Pour banana mixture evenly into ramekins. Place ramekins in a 13- x 9- x 2-inch baking pan; add hot water to baking pan to depth of 1 inch. Bake at 350° for 50 minutes or until set. Remove ramekins from pan; cool. Cover and chill 8 hours.

Loosen edges of custards with a knife or rubber spatula. Invert ramekins onto dessert plates; garnish with mint sprigs, if desired. Yield: 6 servings.

PER SERVING: 294 CALORIES (16% FROM FAT)
FAT 5.2G (SATURATED FAT 2.1G)
PROTEIN 7.2G CARBOHYDRATE 54.8G
CHOLESTEROL 154MG SODIUM 85MG

Banana-Caramel Custard

BAKED EGG CUSTARD

3 cups 2% low-fat milk
2 eggs
2 egg whites
¼ cup sugar
¼ cup firmly packed brown sugar
2 teaspoons vanilla extract
½ teaspoon almond extract
¼ teaspoon ground nutmeg

Heat milk in a heavy saucepan over medium-high heat to 180° or until tiny bubbles form around edge of pan (do not boil). Remove from heat.

Combine eggs and egg whites in a large bowl; beat well with a wire whisk. Add sugars; beat well with a wire whisk. Gradually add milk to egg mixture, beating constantly. Stir in flavorings.

Pour ½ cup egg mixture into each of eight 6-ounce custard cups; sprinkle with nutmeg. Place four custard cups in each of two 9-inch round cakepans; add hot water to each pan to a depth of 1 inch. Bake at 325° for 45 minutes or until set. Remove custard cups from pans; cool to room temperature. Cover with plastic wrap; chill. Yield: 8 servings.

PER SERVING: 124 CALORIES (23% FROM FAT)
FAT 3.1G (SATURATED FAT 1.5G)
PROTEIN 5.5G CARBOHYDRATE 17.9G
CHOLESTEROL 63MG SODIUM 77MG

CITRUS SPONGE PUDDING

As it bakes, this dessert forms two layers—a creamy pudding nestled beneath a spongy cake top.

1 cup 1% low-fat milk
½ cup unsweetened pineapple juice
2 tablespoons stick margarine, melted
1 teaspoon grated orange rind
1 teaspoon grated lemon rind
⅓ cup fresh lemon juice
3 egg yolks
¾ cup sugar
⅓ cup all-purpose flour
¼ teaspoon salt
3 egg whites
Vegetable cooking spray
1 teaspoon powdered sugar

Combine first 7 ingredients in a large bowl, stirring with a wire whisk; set aside. Combine ¾ cup sugar, flour, and salt. Gradually add milk mixture, stirring well (batter will be thin).

Beat egg whites at high speed of an electric mixer until stiff peaks form. Gently stir one-fourth of egg whites into batter; gently fold in remaining egg whites.

Pour batter into a 1½-quart casserole dish coated with cooking spray. Place casserole dish in an 8-inch square baking dish; add hot water to baking dish to a depth of 1 inch. Bake at 350° for 50 minutes or until golden. Sprinkle with powdered sugar. Serve warm or chilled. Yield: 6 servings.

PER SERVING: 227 CALORIES (28% FROM FAT)
FAT 7.0G (SATURATED FAT 1.8G)
PROTEIN 5.3G   CARBOHYDRATE 36.7G
CHOLESTEROL 111MG   SODIUM 194MG

LEMON BREAD PUDDING WITH BLACKBERRY SAUCE

The tangy pudding in this lemon-lovers' delight provides a nice contrast to the sweet blackberry sauce.

1 cup sugar, divided
2 cups nonfat buttermilk
¾ cup fat-free egg substitute
2 teaspoons grated lemon rind
⅓ cup fresh lemon juice
2 tablespoons stick margarine, melted
8 (1-ounce) slices French bread, cut into 1-inch cubes
1 (16-ounce) package frozen unsweetened blackberries, thawed
Vegetable cooking spray

Combine ¾ cup sugar and next 6 ingredients in a large bowl; toss gently. Cover and chill 1 hour.

Combine remaining ¼ cup sugar and blackberries in container of an electric blender; cover and process until smooth. Set aside.

Spoon bread mixture into an 11- x 7- x 2-inch baking dish coated with cooking spray. Bake at 350° for 40 minutes or until set. Serve warm or at room temperature. To serve, top ½ cup pudding with about 3 tablespoons blackberry sauce. Yield: 9 servings.

PER SERVING: 240 CALORIES (13% FROM FAT)
FAT 3.5G (SATURATED FAT 0.8G)
PROTEIN 6.7G   CARBOHYDRATE 46.5G
CHOLESTEROL 3MG   SODIUM 263MG

Pumpkin Flan

PUMPKIN FLAN

1 cup sugar, divided
1 (16-ounce) can pumpkin
1 teaspoon pumpkin pie spice
1 teaspoon vanilla extract
½ teaspoon maple extract
½ cup skim milk
¼ cup unsweetened orange juice
4 egg whites, lightly beaten
2 egg yolks, lightly beaten
1 (12-ounce) can evaporated skimmed milk
Cinnamon sticks (optional)
Orange rind curls (optional)

Place ½ cup sugar in a saucepan. Cook over medium heat, stirring constantly, until sugar melts and is light brown. Pour melted sugar into a 10-inch pieplate, tilting to coat bottom; set aside.

Combine remaining ½ cup sugar, pumpkin, and next 3 ingredients, stirring well. Add skim milk and next 4 ingredients; stir well. Pour pumpkin mixture into prepared pieplate; place in a large shallow pan. Pour hot water into pan to depth of 1 inch.

Bake at 350° for 1 hour and 5 minutes or until a knife inserted in center of flan comes out clean. Remove pieplate from water; cool flan in pieplate on a wire rack.

Cover and chill at least 4 hours. Loosen edges of flan with a knife; invert onto a rimmed serving plate. If desired, garnish with cinnamon sticks and orange rind curls. Yield: 8 servings.

PER SERVING: 184 CALORIES (8% FROM FAT)
FAT 1.6G (SATURATED FAT 0.6G)
PROTEIN 6.8G   CARBOHYDRATE 36.0G
CHOLESTEROL 56MG   SODIUM 88MG

CHILLED CHOCOLATE-BANANA SOUFFLÉ

Once this soufflé chills, it deflates and takes on the consistency of mousse or baked pudding.

Vegetable cooking spray
½ cup plus 2 teaspoons sugar, divided
¼ cup all-purpose flour
3 tablespoons unsweetened cocoa
1 cup 1% low-fat milk
2 egg yolks
½ cup mashed ripe banana
1 tablespoon stick margarine, melted
1 tablespoon dark rum
1 teaspoon vanilla extract
6 large egg whites
¼ teaspoon salt
2 tablespoons sugar
½ cup frozen reduced-calorie whipped topping, thawed

Coat a 2-quart soufflé dish with cooking spray; sprinkle with 2 teaspoons sugar. Set aside.

Combine ½ cup sugar, flour, and cocoa in a saucepan; add milk, stirring with a wire whisk until blended. Cook over medium heat 5 minutes or until thick and bubbly, stirring constantly.

Beat yolks in a large bowl with whisk. Gradually add chocolate mixture to yolks, whisking constantly. Stir in banana and next 3 ingredients.

Beat egg whites and salt at high speed of an electric mixer until foamy. Add 2 tablespoons sugar, 1 tablespoon at a time, beating until stiff peaks form. Gently fold one-fourth of egg white mixture into chocolate mixture; gently fold in remaining egg white mixture. Spoon into prepared soufflé dish.

Place soufflé dish in a 9-inch square baking pan; add hot water to pan to a depth of 1 inch. Bake at 350° for 55 minutes or until puffy and set. Remove from water; cool to room temperature. Cover and chill 8 hours. Top each serving with 1 tablespoon whipped topping. Yield: 8 servings.

PER SERVING: 169 CALORIES (21% FROM FAT)
FAT 4.0G (SATURATED FAT 1.5G)
PROTEIN 5.5G CARBOHYDRATE 26.7G
CHOLESTEROL 56MG SODIUM 151MG

FUDGE SOUFFLÉ CAKE WITH TURTLE SAUCE

Butter-flavored vegetable cooking spray
¼ teaspoon sugar
½ cup unsweetened cocoa
¼ cup plus 2 tablespoons hot water
2 tablespoons stick margarine
3 tablespoons all-purpose flour
¾ cup 1% low-fat milk
¼ cup sugar
⅛ teaspoon salt
4 large egg whites
3 tablespoons sugar
Turtle Sauce

Coat a 1½-quart souffle dish with cooking spray; sprinkle with ¼ teaspoon sugar. Set aside.

Combine cocoa and hot water. Stir well; set aside.

Melt margarine in a small heavy saucepan over medium heat. Add flour; cook, stirring constantly with a wire whisk, 1 minute. Add milk, ¼ cup sugar, and salt; cook 3 minutes or until thickened, stirring constantly. Remove from heat. Add cocoa mixture; stir well. Spoon into a large bowl; cool slightly.

Beat egg whites at high speed of an electric mixer until foamy. Add 3 tablespoons sugar, 1 tablespoon at a time, beating until stiff peaks form. Gently fold 1 cup egg white mixture into cocoa mixture; gently fold in remaining egg white mixture. Spoon into prepared soufflé dish.

Bake at 375° for 35 minutes or until puffy and set. Remove from oven; serve warm, at room temperature, or chilled. Top each serving with about 1 tablespoon Turtle Sauce. Yield: 6 servings.

TURTLE SAUCE
¼ cup plus 2 tablespoons fat-free caramel-flavored sundae syrup
3 tablespoons chopped pecans, toasted

Place caramel syrup in a bowl; microwave at HIGH 30 seconds. Stir in pecans. Yield: ½ cup.

PER SERVING: 241 CALORIES (29% FROM FAT)
FAT 7.8G (SATURATED FAT 1.7G)
PROTEIN 6.1G CARBOHYDRATE 58.6G
CHOLESTEROL 2MG SODIUM 182MG

Individual Apricot Soufflés

INDIVIDUAL APRICOT SOUFFLÉS

Vegetable cooking spray
4 large egg whites
1½ tablespoons plus 1 teaspoon sugar, divided
½ cup Apricot Puree
½ teaspoon vanilla extract

Coat bottom of six 4-ounce ramekins lightly with cooking spray; set aside.

Beat egg whites at high speed of an electric mixer until foamy. Gradually add 1½ tablespoons sugar, beating until stiff peaks form.

Combine Apricot Puree and vanilla in a large bowl; stir well. Gently stir one-fourth of egg white mixture into apricot mixture. Gently fold remaining egg white mixture into apricot mixture. Spoon into prepared ramekins, and sprinkle with remaining 1 teaspoon sugar. Bake at 400° for 10 minutes. Serve immediately. Yield: 6 servings.

APRICOT PUREE
1 (3-ounce) package dried apricots
½ cup water

Combine apricots and water in a small saucepan; cover and cook over low heat 20 minutes.

Position knife blade in food processor bowl; add apricot mixture. Process until smooth, scraping sides of bowl with a rubber spatula. Yield: ½ cup.

PER SERVING: 62 CALORIES (6% FROM FAT)
FAT 0.4G (SATURATED FAT 0.0G)
PROTEIN 2.7G CARBOHYDRATE 12.4G
CHOLESTEROL 0MG SODIUM 45MG